Parents Empowered

Healing and deliverance with kids and teens

Daniel and Esther Baumgartner

Bethesda Heilungsdienst

Title: Parents Empowered: Healing and deliverance with kids and teens
First Edition.
Copyright:© 2019 Daniel Baumgartner and Esther Baumgartner All rights reserved.

No part of this publication may be reproduced, distributed, or transmitted in any form or by any means, including photocopying, recording, or any other electronic or mechanical methods, without the prior written permission of the authors, except in the case of brief quotations embodied in reviews and certain other non-commercial uses permitted by copyright law.

Print: ISBN 978-3-9525127-0-8

ebook: ISBN 978-3-9525127-1-5

Published by: Verein Bethesda Heilungsdienst
Stapferstrasse 29
8006, Zürich
Switzerland
info@bethesda-heilungsdienst.ch

Distribution: See internet for current info
Internet: www.bethesda-heilungsdienst.ch

Scriptures: Scriptures taken from the Holy Bible, New International Version®, NIV®.
Copyright © 1973, 1978, 1984, 2011 by Biblica, Inc.™
Used by permission of Zondervan. All rights reserved worldwide.
www.zondervan.com. The "NIV" and "New International Version" are trademarks registered in the United States Patent and Trademark Office by Biblica, Inc.™

Editorial & design: David M.Taylor, SoundsWrite GmbH, Switzerland. www.soundswrite.ch,

Illustrations: Claudia Huber, www.claudiahuber-illustration.de

Proof-reading: Adger Mackay, Elisabeth Taylor

Disclaimer   The names of children, teens and adults cited in the real examples have been changed to protect their confidentiality. Noah and Nick, Anna and Marie are generic examples, based on our extensive prayer ministry experience. Reference to children can be taken to include teens, unless otherwise stated. Parents are responsible for adapting the material to suit their child's age, developmental level and individual situation.

This is a self-help book with advice on parenting. It assumes a spiritual world-view that is consistent with the teachings of the New Testament. Prayer for deliverance has been practiced by followers of Christ throughout history. It has always been a controversial topic. Readers must exercise discernment in the way they apply the contents of this book as well as the way they communicate the insights contained herein. The authors and Bethesda Heilungsdienst disclaim responsibility for any loss, damage, or disruption due to errors or omissions in the information and advice given in this book, whether such errors or omissions result from negligence, accident, or any other cause.

The authors insist on the importance of accurately discerning the difference between spiritual, emotional and physical issues and explicitly advise readers to take into account the advice of relevant specialists including doctors, child psychiatrists or teachers.

Endorsements

"Daniel and Esther Baumgartner have written a must-read guide for parents. It encompasses not only detailed practical ways to establish a healthy interaction with your children, including confronting a variety of difficult situations they can encounter, but also offers anointed teaching on deliverance from demonic oppression which can invade a child's life. An extremely worthwhile read."
– Susan Banks, Co-author of "Deliverance for Children and Teens", Impact Christian Books, Inc. USA

"Parents Empowered is a book for our times. Many parents struggle to understand their children's problems and behaviour, and are subsequently unsure how to help them. Others want tools to help their children grow up to be healthy, balanced adults, properly equipped to face the challenges of life. Parents Empowered is such a tool. It is easy to read and understand and amusingly illustrated. The content reflects the authors' deep Bible knowledge and long-standing, solid practical experience and burning desire to help each parent and every child find the joy and richness in life meant for them. Both parents and those working with kids outside the home will find this a valuable resource."*– Pastors Pekka and Anneli Tommola, Ruach Ministries, Finland*

"I have admired the ministry Daniel and Esther have had for years helping people to overcome their problems, many of which started in childhood. I have seen their three sons flourish as they used these principles. I am delighted to endorse this comprehensive, easy to read book as an extension of a second generation ministry. I am sure it will enable parents around the world to understand, pray with and help their children grow up to be emotionally and spiritually mature by learning to deal with hurts, sins and their reactions in the way God intended and made possible through Christ's sacrifice for us." *– Dr Pam Williams, G.P., Australia*

"I am excited about this book because it offers parents a simple tool box they can understand and actually use to help their children overcome hurts and a variety of other problems as well. Daniel and Esther deal with important and difficult issues in a clear, competent manner. Their recommendations and steps offered are anchored in the Bible, and the many practical examples help the reader visualise the approach. The teaching on how children can be influenced by demonic spirits when natural protective barriers are broken is also very important and shows the need to pray with children at a deep level.

I first met Daniel Baumgartner and his parents-in-law, Albert and Elisabeth Taylor, authors of "Ministering Below the Surface," many years ago and received much healing through them. This made a real difference in my life, and I have used what I learned from them about healing and deliverance with my Christian clients where appropriate.

Even if you are not yet familiar with deliverance ministry, I recommend giving this book a chance. A lot of prayer has gone into it, and readers are bound to experience the Holy Spirit moving in their own lives as they work through the guide." – *Dr Mikaela Blomqvist-Lyytikäinen, Child and Adolescent Psychiatrist, Finland*

"Christian parents are desperate for help in raising kids who truly know the power of God's Word, walk in His ways and experience victory over the onslaughts of today's evils. "Parents Empowered" is a vitally important tool, unlike anything we've seen before, to help parents do this. Readers will discover that children can be trained and trusted to navigate life's hurtful and harmful experiences – God's way. His adult children will also derive transforming benefits as they pursue healing and wholeness in Christ for their children. This is a book sure to create a Kingdom impact. We look forward to its roots spreading deep and wide." – *Jacqueline and Tanie Guy, Founding Directors of Forget-Me-not-Ministries, USA*

Foreword

Writing the forward for your daughter's book will make any mother proud, because aren't we parents our children's greatest fans? Yet writing this hasn't been that easy as I find myself feeling almost jealous of you lucky readers.

You see, I wish I had known everything you can read in this book when Esther and her brothers were born. Instead, my husband and I had to learn much of what we now know through painful and perplexing experiences. However, as we pressed in to understand the realms of inner healing and deliverance, we were able to avoid some of the worst outcomes that we have seen in our own ministry as missionaries and counsellors.

My late husband, Albert and I worked together with Daniel and Esther over many years. As young people they accompanied us on our international ministry trips, teaching and praying for many. They have seen thousands of lives healed and transformed over the last twenty-five years. Daniel translated our own book, "Ministering Below the Surface" into his native German. The material is a foundational part of their teaching and approach to parenting.

Now, drawing on their own family life and ministry, Daniel and Esther share many practical examples which bring the material to life. The clear prayer steps empower and equip the reader to effectively minister to his or her own child.

Esther, you are a wonderful daughter to me, particularly now that I am on my own; Daniel, an exemplary son-in-law, supporting me in so many practical ways. My three Baumgartner grandchildren, each one precious to me, bring me great joy.

Holy Spirit, thank you that you always lead us into your truth and give us your wisdom. Thank you for all you are doing in our family.

Elisabeth Taylor, Co-author of "Ministering Below the Surface."

Acknowledgements

Daniel and Esther Baumgartner would like to thank:

Our three sons, Benjamin, Samuel and Peter. Each one precious. You've allowed us to talk about your lives and share some of your individual stories so others can benefit. This is both courageous and gracious.

Elisabeth Taylor and her late husband Albert. You have been parents and grandparents who made a difference. We have learned much from you. Our steps to healing and freedom for children and teens are based on your approach.

David M. Taylor. As writing coach and editor your input has been invaluable. Top in your field, we've learned an infinite amount from you, and been equipped to communicate our message. Your production design makes the book accessible and a pleasure to read. Your unwavering brotherly and spiritual support are a great blessing. We couldn't have done it without you.

Claudia Huber. Your inspired illustrations add a valuable dimension to the work, bringing the message to life with great humour and skill.

Adger McKay. Working with you in the final writing stage has been a real blessing. Your positive and gentle approach are an example to us.

Our friends and partners at Bethesda Heilungsdienst. Your love, prayers and generosity over so many years have enabled us to keep going.

Above all our loving Heavenly Father. Author of parenthood. The ultimate source of healing and freedom. We cannot thank you enough for what you have done for us as individuals and as a family. Thank you for enabling us to share with you in this ministry.

Introduction

Parenting has never been easy, and the modern world hasn't made it easier. We have so many different roles to play at work and at home, and the job of parenting is probably the one job we never got trained for. It is easy to feel overwhelmed: too much is at stake if we 'get it wrong'. So more and more people are leaving their job to the 'experts'. The result is a tragic loss of heart-to-heart relationship, confidence and power in Christian parenting and homes today.

But what if there was another approach? What if God has uniquely chosen and positioned you, *Christian parent*, to make the difference in your child's life? What if he has equipped you with spiritual tools to discern what is bothering your child and effectively help your child overcome many issues yourself? We believe he has!

In our experience, many of the roots of emotional, spiritual and physical problems facing children and teens today can be found in three key areas: emotional hurts, unresolved sin and demonic oppression. If left untreated, issues in any of these inter-connected areas can power destructive behaviour, attitudes and poor choices – now and into adulthood. But healthy foundations for life are laid when children learn to deal swiftly and effectively with issues in each of these areas.

In this step-by-step guide, we show you how to do this, starting with (re-) building a heart-to-heart relationship with your child and making your home a place where healing can happen and freedom be experienced. We go on to offer practical, easy-to-follow, age-adaptable spiritual tools to heal emotional pain in children and help them overcome their own negative reactions to hurt. You will discover how to help your child deal with sin, forgive others and receive forgiveness without lowering their self-esteem. You will learn how to identify and set your child free from demonic attack and oppression, so that your child can go on to enjoy life to the full.

We have used this approach for more than twenty-five years, helping children and adults, from a wide variety of social backgrounds on different continents, to overcome issues and (re-)lay healthy foundations in their lives. It has also powered our own parenting – with amazing results. Indeed, we are convinced that the emotional, physical and spiritual health our three teenage boys enjoy today, is largely due to having applied and taught them the very keys we share with you here.

Whether you are a first-time parent, wanting to give your unborn child the best possible start in life, the parent of a young child or teen struggling with issues, or simply involved in raising children, applying the insights and prayers with confidence will revolutionise your approach. The five prayers are rooted in the teachings of the Bible, and available to us in Jesus Christ. They are easy to grasp, simple to use and effective. You can apply them to help your child deal with a specific crisis or issue at hand, such as trauma, loss or sickness. Or simply use them on a day-to-day level to teach your child how to keep spiritually and emotionally fit. As you get used to using these tools, you and your child will be better equipped to deal with the challenges of life and parenting both great and small.

You will benefit most by reading through the whole book to gain an overview of the relationship between hurts, sin and the demonic. Then work through each chapter, using the 'pause for thought' questions to help you apply the material to your own situation. Keep a journal to record the changes in your home as a result of using your spiritual tools. This will encourage you to keep pressing forward. Our prayer is that, as you discover, apply and re-apply the tools in this book, you too will have the joy of seeing your child grow up to prosper, even as their soul prospers.

Overview of prayers for flourishing kids

The hurts prayers

Emotional healing for simple hurts

p. 51

The reactions prayers

Healthy responses instead of damaging developments

p. 60

The memories prayers

Dealing with past incidents

p. 65

The forgiveness prayers

Getting right and cleaning up our mess

p.76

The freedom prayers

Deliverance / dealing with
spiritual infection

p. 96

Help for you and your children

The spiritual tools presented in this book can work with kids of all ages: simply adapt the language. You can bring both yourself and your child to Jesus and allow him to heal your hurts and bring you both through to wholeness and freedom!

Contents

You can make the difference !
A.

YOU CAN MAKE THE DIFFER- ENCE !

1. God wants your child to flourish
You can make the difference

We celebrated the news that we were going to be parents with a glass of sparkling wine that Daniel spotted in a corner of our local northern Argentine supermarket. Probably not the wisest choice of beverage when you've just discovered you're pregnant, but we were young and just super-excited!

It was the days of snail mail, and a dial-up internet so slow you could learn multiple languages just waiting for a connection. So our preparations for parenthood centred largely on books inherited from previous missionaries and visitors passing through. We had two on pregnancy. One was a brightly coloured illustration charting the progress of our unborn child in the womb. I (Esther) read and re-read with awe the tips and advice on how to prepare for birth and care for a newborn baby. But, we didn't talk much as a couple about what kind of parents we wanted to be. Or what *approach* to parenting we would adopt when the child actually arrived.

Ours was a multi-cultural home: Daniel is Swiss and I am British/Swiss and we would be raising the family in a third culture – Argentina. So as far as cultural questions go, more discussion ahead of time would certainly have helped smooth our parenting path! However, we did agree on one thing: we would pray for our children – right from the womb – using the spiritual insights and prayers which had changed our own lives, time and time again. And we would teach them how to use these prayers for themselves from an early age.

As we look back on two decades of parenting, we haven't been perfect parents – but we have had the joy of helping our three boys become emotionally, spiritually and physically strong. Because each time the need arose and we prayed the healing and freedom prayers with them, we saw visible changes in their behaviour and attitudes. Today, they are flourishing young people. Not only do they know and love their God, but they have experienced his power. They have learned to use these prayers at a daily level to deal with the reality of hurt, sin and demonic attack in their own lives.

Chosen, positioned and equipped

As a parent, you have a relationship with your child that no-one else on this planet shares. God has given you this gift. He has designed this relationship to bring great mutual joy. He has chosen this framework for teaching your child to know and love God intimately and follow him closely – all their days.[1] God himself models this; he is both father and mother to his children. Parenthood and relationship, therefore, are at the very heart of who God himself is.

Not only has God chosen you, but he has also positioned you to know your child deeply in a way no one else can. Your proximity to your child enables you to detect changes in them and their environment, which others might miss. And these changes might just be keys to what is really going on in their life and what their true needs are.

God has equipped you for the job that he has entrusted you with: if you are a born again follower of Christ, you have his very mind, his wisdom and his authority. The same power that raised Christ from the dead is at work in you. His healing power can flow through you to meet *whatever* needs your child may have, whether it be physical, emotional or spiritual. He can use you to make the difference.[2] These are spiritual truths and we need to start to build on them, even when our feelings tell us something else.

Daniel and I have had plenty of struggles of our own, but we were simply determined to use the spiritual tools in our hands. We chose to be confident that God would lead us and use us to help our children deal with whatever life threw at them. We were also hungry to learn more. And to the best of our knowledge, we were wholeheartedly committed and surrendered to the Lord.

---

1   See Deuteronomy 6:5-9; Proverbs 22:6; Ephesians 6:4
2   Read John 3:16; Ephesians 1:19; 1 Corinthians 2:14-16; Matthew 28:18-19; Matthew 10:8

You can do it!

There is a spiritual dimension to this world and emotional and spiritual dimensions to situations experienced in the physical realm. In our experience, many emotional, spiritual and even physical problems children and teens face have their roots in emotional hurt, painful memories, negative reactions to hurt; or in sin that has not been dealt with and in demonic powers that have gained access to their lives. God wants to show us these roots, and the cross empowers us to deal with them effectively.

God is the source of healing and freedom – even in the face of the greatest difficulties. If we stay plugged into him, he will guide, lead and use us to bring his healing and freedom to our children.

So, if you sense, or perhaps know for a fact, that your child needs help dealing with inner hurts and pain, struggles with sin or is under demonic attack or bondage, be encouraged. God has positioned and equipped you, Christian parent, to heal and bring them freedom! He is for you. He loves your child and wants them whole!

As you learn to apply the insights and prayers we share in this book with increasing confidence and authority, adapting them appropriately to fit your child's age and circumstances, you will be amazed at the difference it makes to their lives and the atmosphere in your home in general. And in doing so, you will be helping your child lay the emotional, spiritual and physical foundations they need to flourish.

> **Pause for thought**
>
> What kind of parent do you want to be?
>
> Thank God that he has uniquely chosen, positioned and equipped you to help your child flourish!

2. A quality of life beyond your wildest dreams

God's original plan and heart was for every child to grow up with both father and mother in a loving, stable, safe and faith-filled home. Clearly, many children today are growing up in less-than-ideal, sometimes excruciatingly challenging circumstances. They may have experienced death, divorce, or be surrounded by strife, contention or instability on a daily level. Others may be deeply lonely.

Whatever the circumstances, however dark the darkness, however deep the pain a child is going through, God cares about your child. He sees their hurts, struggles and pain. He sees where they are bound and long to be free. The Bible says that all of human beings are so valuable to God, that even the hairs on our head are numbered (Luke 12:7). We also read that the Lord knits us together in our mother's womb (Psalm 139:13). He knows us by name (Isaiah 43:1). All of these verses apply to your child!

If you are a Christian, you will have heard that Jesus Christ dealt with your sin and the sin of the world on the cross. But that is not just a promise for when you die. God's desire is to give us more than a theological 'get out of jail free card' and being a Christian parent means more than being able to bring your kids to playgroup, or being able to drop them off for Sunday school or some exciting summer camp.

There is much more to this great adventure that God has invited you to. God actually cares about you and your children individually. He cares about your hurts and problems and he wants you to be heavily involved in the process of making this world a better place, where everyone can live life to the full.

Life to the full

As Christians we know that Jesus saves or that he came to save. But many are not aware that this salvation includes fullness of life and also healing.

Consider Christ's words: *"I have come that they may have life, and have it to the full"* (John 10:10). When we look at what Jesus did throughout his ministry, we see what he meant by this. He healed people, he delivered them, he taught them and he even fed them. So the fullness of life that Jesus is talking about refers to being healthy, free and having our natural needs met. Note that the Greek word for salvation, 'soteria' is translated as 'healing' in examples like these:

- A sick woman, who had an issue of blood for twelve years says to herself: *"'If I only touch his cloak, I will be healed.' Jesus turned and saw her. 'Take heart, daughter,' he said, 'your faith has healed you.' And the woman was healed at that moment."* (Matthew 9:21-22).
- Jairus' little daughter was dying, so he begs Jesus to help: *"Please come and put your hands on her so that she will be healed and live."* (Mark 5:23)

Now besides demonstrating God's heart for adults and children to have fullness of life, Jesus also taught his followers to be people who heal and deliver. He promised the Holy Spirit so that believers can be empowered to deal with whatever stops us and our children experiencing full or abundant life. When you learn to deal with things like hurts, sins and demonic attack – by the power of the Holy Spirit, you can enjoy a quality of life that right now may seem to be beyond your wildest dreams.

So, if you are wondering who to turn to for help with whatever is bothering your child, then turn to God first! He knows and loves them. He wants to put a smile back on their face. God demonstrated his love and commitment to us by coming down to our level, taking the form of a man and going through the agony of the cross. Jesus endured the cross because he had some people in mind – namely you and your children (Hebrews 12:2)! He wanted to see you all saved, healed and living in full freedom.

His resurrection from the dead is the ultimate victory over every power that is between us and abundant life.

Stories of turn-arounds

The odds of flourishing were heavily stacked against Natalie, born to a sixteen-year-old in an unspectacular Swiss suburb. But godly grandparents helped raise her. When Natalie was a teen, they talked with her about the rejection that had surrounded her birth. Their involvement and constant prayers forever changed their granddaughter's destiny. Today she is a beautiful young college student embracing life and living it with joy.

Tanya grew up in Scandinavia with an emotionally distant mother and a father who suffered from bipolar. But she was blessed to have her great-grandmother living with them: "Her presence and prayers made growing up in that situation more bearable for me. I was devastated when I lost her in my early teens, but she paved the way for me to find Christ as an adult."

Pause for thought

Do you believe your child is valued and loved by God and that he sees your situation?

Thank God for the cross and that he wants to use you to bring wholeness to your child.

3. Stories from the battlefield

How we sharpened our weapons

In this book, we are going to share with you plenty of true stories from our own experiences as parents and prayer counsellors. Our hope is that you will be encouraged and inspired. Some incidents may seem strange to you, particularly if you are unfamiliar with the unseen, spiritual realm, as many Westerners are. Nevertheless, please keep an open mind because what we share here may be the key to unlocking a situation you face in your home now or in the future.

Prayer turns our son's birth around

We bathed our first born son in prayer from conception and as he grew in the womb. We prayed for his general health, development and protection. We prayed that God's love and presence would fill him. But we also prayed specifically against inherited allergies and other illnesses which we knew to be present on both or either side of the family.[3]

Apart from persistent nausea, the pregnancy was progressing well. Our baby was due to be born any day and we were ready for him! So when the doctor gravely informed us that we were in for a long, painful birth or even a caesarian section, we were shocked. Apparently, our little one was facing feet rather than head down. This breech position was not good news. "Will the baby not turn on its own? Could you perhaps turn him?" we asked anxiously. We so wanted a natural birth! The doctor replied, "In my experience, it is highly unlikely he will turn again at this stage. I can't risk turning him manually either, because if the umbilical cord winds around his neck, it could cut off his oxygen supply."

It hit us that we had a choice: accept what was happening in the natural, or fight it in the spiritual realm. We had spent months praying for a good, natural delivery. We knew that severe pain in childbirth was not what God

---

3   We talk more about praying for your unborn child in the Extras.

originally intended for women, but was a consequence of the fall of mankind. We believed that Jesus carried all our pains and broke every curse when he became a curse for us on the cross. So we knew that the prognosis of a particularly long and painful birth could not be God's best for us. We concluded that it must be a direct assault on the abundant life Jesus died to give us.[4]

We decided to pray. To banish fear and exercise faith for a miracle. Laying his hands on Esther's tummy, Daniel took authority over every demonic attack trying to interfere with our son's birth and commanded every spirit involved to go. Esther yawned a couple of times.[5] He then spoke to the baby, and told him to come into the right position for birth in the Name of Jesus Christ. As he prayed, we felt movement in the womb and knew God was working. When the same doctor examined Esther two days later, he was astonished to find that the baby was indeed back in perfect position! When it came to it, the labour and birth was so swift and easy that Ben almost ended up being born in the car on the way to hospital!

Blockage to conception removed

When the time came to think about a second child, the Lord showed us that he was giving us another son, Samuel. But unlike with our first child, conceived swiftly, something seemed to be stopping Samuel coming. We asked the Lord how to pray. We remembered that Esther's mother had also had some hindrances to conceiving her second child. We sensed the same spiritual blockage stopping Esther conceiving as well. As we prayed and cut Esther loose from this in the spiritual realm, she felt a pressure in her stomach, which then left. The following month she became pregnant! Needless to say, it was another boy, whom of course we named Samuel. This incident showed us that there can be things in our lives stopping us receiving the good things the Lord wants to give us. We can pray and ask him to show us what these are and then pray to remove them.

---

4   See Genesis 3:16, Gal. 3:13 and Isaiah 53:4
5   Yawning often happens during freedom prayers – the Bible word for a spirit is a breath.

Setting our baby free from fear

Daniel was watching a wildlife documentary one day with our six-month-old son sleeping peacefully in the pram beside him. When a huge crocodile opened its terrifying jaws, Daniel glanced over at our baby and was surprised to find that he was now wide awake and staring at the TV screen. Suddenly, he began crying frantically and nothing Daniel did calmed him. Getting him back off to sleep was out of the question. Unsure what to do next, Daniel prayed for wisdom. He sensed that a demonic spirit was attacking his baby son and that he should tell it to go. As he did this, a look of terror came over the infant's face, as the spirit of fear showed itself and left. His features relaxed, his eyes closed and he immediately fell asleep!

As we thought about this incident over the years, we often wondered what would have happened if that spirit of fear had been allowed to stay and take root in our son's life. We couldn't explain everything that happened on a human or developmental level, but spiritually-speaking it made sense. You see, there is a battle going on over our children. And just as in any war, the enemy does not play fair. He comes to steal, kill and destroy in whatever way he can, whatever chance he gets; but Jesus has come to bring life in abundance (John 10:10). This incident confirmed to us the need to be prepared and integrate healing and freedom into everyday parenting.

Delivering our young child from impurity

Believe it or not, some kids still grow up in a world where it is normal to play in the middle of the street and roam around with other kids. Ours were such kids. Play was loosely supervised by the older kids and everyone popped in and out of each other's houses. In a quiet Argentine suburb, with very little traffic it seemed safe enough. One day, however, we noticed something different about our five-year-old son when he came inside. His eyes seemed restless; when we looked into them, he did not seem himself. We asked him if anything had happened and he said no. But from his behaviour over the next few days, it became clear to us that he must have come under the influence of some kind of impure spirit. It turned out that our son had seen a sex scene on TV at a neighbour's house and a spirit of impurity from that film had tried to latch onto him. We explained to him that we could tell the nasty thing which was upsetting him, to go away in Jesus' Name. He agreed, but when we did this, he slipped under the bed and shouted for us to go away. Undeterred, we stood our ground and continued to pray. Calmly and firmly we rebuked the spirit attacking him and commanded it to go. A minute or so later he crawled back out from under the bed and climbed onto Daniel's lap. When we looked into his eyes they were totally peaceful – he was himself once more! We praised the Lord that we had known how to detect and deal with this demonic attack before the spirit really gained a foothold and began to entwine with his developing personality.

Incorporating healing and freedom prayers into everyday life

Experiences of setting our children free became part of everyday life as our children grew. We cultivated the habit of asking the Holy Spirit for guidance as to *how* to pray or *what* to do, whenever we noticed our children were no longer flourishing in a given area of their lives. Each time we saw visible change when we prayed healing and freedom prayers as the Lord led us.

Today, our boys are emotionally, spiritually and physically strong teens and young adults. It's not that they have had an easy ride. On the contrary, they have undergone tremendous challenges, including moving from provincial Northern Argentina to a busy Swiss metropolis. However, they are learning to deal with emotional hurts, sin and demonic attack – God's way. Our prayer is that the stories and insights we share in this book will inspire and empower you to minister to and equip your child with the spiritual tools they need to thrive, as well.

Pause for thought

What are some of your own stories?

Are you facing a "battlefield" situation in your home at the moment? Ask God to equip and prepare you to help your child overcome present and future challenges.

4. Fight today to dance tomorrow

Why children need healing and freedom prayers

When our boys were growing up, we were working in Northern Argentina training adults and building up a number of programmes for children. Invariably, we found ourselves helping people to deal with issues in their personal lives. Again and again we found that these problems had their roots in childhood – in hurtful experiences, painful relationships or traumas. Some people's lives were such a mess, it felt like trying to unravel a huge ball of wool the cat had got hold of and was just as time-consuming! Because without adequate help, just as natural wounds which are left untreated can become infected, so the wounds of childhood fester and become strongholds, powering poor choices, ungodly life-styles and attitudes and yet more difficult relationships.

Many problems can be avoided

We began to ask ourselves, what these people's lives would look like today if they had been helped *as children* to overcome the hurts and traumas as soon as they occurred? What kind of character would they display now, if they had learned God's way of reacting to hurt as children, instead of allowing bitterness, hatred and unforgiveness to take root and fester in their hearts? How much pain and suffering could have been avoided if they had been set free from demonic spirits as soon as they tried to invade their lives, rather than leaving them to take root and become strongholds?

And what of the many hurting children around us in the Sunday schools and day-care centres? Could they be healed and set free using the same prayer tools we used with adults and adapted to our own kids? Could their futures look different as well?

We soon had a chance to find out when we were enlisted to help at a day-care centre in Jujuy, a neighbouring province. The centre was run by some sisters and a Christian psychologist who were observing cycles of generational suffering and felt that healing and freedom prayers could be the answer to breaking the tragic cycles of abuse, unwanted pregnancies, abandonment, poverty, etc. that were being repeated from one generation to the next. As we began ministering to these kids we saw that healing and freedom prayers can make a real difference immediately and in the long term.

From this and other experiences we began to simply adapt the freedom and healing prayers that we were using when counselling adults to suit the needs and age of our own boys and other children in the churches we were involved with.

Parallels between healing and freedom for adults and children

We all know that as children, we get hurt. But often we were not able to express or deal with our pain. We also do wrong things as kids, but we may not know how to put things right or deal with our guilt. We may come under demonic influence, but not know how to protect ourselves or get free.

A child's spirit can be totally alive to God through Christ, even as their bodies and souls are in the process of maturing. For example, a toddler can worship God just like an adult, but when they don't get their own way they throw a tantrum. They need help learning to control their emotions and body to develop healthily.

So as parents our role is to help our children in all these areas. From the moment a child is able to exercise their will, they should be taught to pray and engage their will to get free and healed as much as possible.[6]

Pause for thought

How might you have benefited from healing and freedom prayers as a child?

Is the concept of a child having a spirit, soul and body new to you? For more info read 1Thessalonians 5:23 and Isaiah 61:1-3.

---

6   See also Adapting prayers for different ages in the Extras.

5. Healthy adults healthy children

Practical and deep level change

Melanie, a single mum brought her eight-year-old son to see us about behavioural problems at school. During counselling it emerged that she was having difficulty setting clear and consistent boundaries – a problem that was rooted in the anger she felt towards her own father. He would zero in on her faults, rarely praising her or offering any encouragement. Melanie had rebelled against this and vowed never to be like her dad. As we prayed, she forgave her father and repented of her own rebellion. Having done this, she began to take back her God-given authority as a mother and learned to establish appropriate boundaries and be consistent in her parenting. The transformation process of mother and son went hand-in-hand.

Heal yourself, heal your child

Like Melanie, you may become aware of areas of your life, affecting your child, that need God's touch. Remember, you don't have to be a professional, a spiritual giant or even a perfect parent to help your child overcome issues using healing and freedom prayers. But you do need to be open to God moving in your own life and be willing to change your approach where necessary.

Many parents are uncomfortable with the idea that they might be part of the problem. It is much easier to point to society, the teacher, other kids, a syndrome or a sickness. Sometimes these explanations are valid. But Jesus said the *truth* will set us free (John. 8:32). Taking an honest look at the situation in your home, past and present behaviour and attitudes is a great place to start. And God is kind and gentle. He does not leave us feeling condemned, but energised with new hope and freedom!

As you think about issues your child struggles with, you may also become aware of parallels to your own biographical experience. Be encouraged, God wants to heal you both! Your child doesn't have to go through what you went through. Prayer changes destinies. In the day-care centre in Jujuy, we saw that cycles of sin and destruction can indeed be broken. Put your faith and trust in Jesus, believing that he can heal you and give your child a brighter future. So, let God treat and heal your wounds, as you open your life to Him and seek healing and wholeness for your child. Rely on His revelation and leading as you pray for and with your child about the things that bother them.

Situations requiring change in practical parenting

While the focus of this book is on issues that require healing and spiritual freedom, some cases simply need practical changes to be made.

Juan (9)

A mother came to see us about her nine-year-old son, who she suspected had ADS (Attention Deficiency Syndrome). As we talked it became clear that she and her husband had very different ideas about how much sleep the boy needed. When asked what time he goes to bed, she was evasive, before finally admitting that she was afraid to impose a routine. As a result the boy was chronically overtired. Rather than freedom or healing prayers, an earlier bedtime was urgently needed.

The second issue was that by staying up late, Juan was seeing things on TV that his young soul was having a hard time processing. Thirdly, the disunity of his parents was a source of deep insecurity and fear. His behaviour was, in part, a reaction to the chaotic, tense environment at home.

Although the basic problem was natural, it must be said that constant arguing in the home does actually add a spiritual dimension. Because, when parents are disunited, it makes their children vulnerable to demonic attack.[7] Whether they liked it or not – for the sake of their son – this couple would have to sit down and reach a consensus on the details of how they would raise their child.

---

7   Derek Prince Ministries, *Instruction On Deliverance For Children And Their Parents*, 1971

Situations requiring deep level healing and freedom

Admitting that our parenting is ineffective because something in our own life is fuelling the fire, is sobering and painful. If we are reacting towards our child from a place of hurt and demonic bondage in our own lives, then no amount of advice on practical parenting will do us much good. But deep level healing and freedom can be the key to change. We share from our own family to illustrate this.

Esther's story

As a child, I suffered frequent unexplainable stomach aches and sometimes wanted to die. I often retreated to a fantasy world of heroic deeds and sexual day dreams. Note that I was growing up in Kenya without TV or magazines that might have triggered such thoughts. As I grew older, the mood swings, insecurity, rejection and isolation increased. When I was seventeen, I talked to a counsellor at a conference about these sexual fantasies and was set free from feelings of shame and guilt. I felt clean and a huge weight was lifted off me. However, it was not until I got married and experienced difficulty opening up to my husband, that the Lord showed me a root of my problems. As a young toddler in Kenya a man tried to abuse me. Daniel prayed with me using the steps for inner healing and freedom.[8] As a result, I was better able to open up sexually and emotionally, but I still experienced mood swings and periods of darkness and despair.

When our first son turned thirteen our relationship dramatically changed. I couldn't understand what was happening to me. I loved him dearly, yet I found myself starting to reject him. I was shocked at the feelings of hatred that emerged in different situations. At times, I wanted to see him suffer. We fought frequently and my son became increasingly rebellious. As his inner pain increased, he began spinning away from us on a downward spiral of destruction. Daniel recognised that something in me still needed to be healed – urgently, before we lost our son.

---

8   See *Ministering below the Surface* by A and E Taylor.

We asked the Lord to show us what the root of the problem poisoning our relationship was. As we prayed, God took me back to an incident, where a young teenage boy abused me sexually at a guest house in Kenya. As a six-year-old, I didn't understand what was happening and my mind immediately locked it away. But when my son turned the approximate age of the boy who had abused me, something inside me was triggered. The memories forced their way to the surface.

I went through the steps to healing of painful memories and freedom with Daniel and came into greater freedom and stability. I also attended a healing retreat in England, and received even more healing from the related depression. One of the visiting priests, who knew nothing about me or my relationship with my son, said to me: "Did you know you represent God to your son? Stop rejecting him. Love him unconditionally, with the love of the Father."

My healing saved my relationship with my son. I stopped rejecting him and began to love and accept him. The change in me, enabled him to open his heart to God again. Today, we have a warm-hearted, close relationship. United with Daniel, we were able to help our son find his way back to a good place. He loves, follows and serves the Lord now with all his heart. I can never thank the Lord enough for what he did for us!

Pause for thought

Are there any practical changes you need to make in your parenting?

Where might your own issues be connected to problems your child is experiencing? Make a decision to work on these.

The healing home

B.

THE HEALING HOME

6. Heart-to-heart relationships

Prioritising the connection

Preachers often use the illustration of the traffic policeman or policewoman to explain the meaning of authority. When you have authority, you can direct traffic to avoid accidents and chaos on the road and it does not require any great effort. So Christian parents have been entrusted with the spiritual authority to instruct and direct their children and avoid chaos in the family.[1] As a parent your primary responsibility is for the family and not the street. The family has a strategic and ordered framework. The father, as head of the family has the promise of the very presence of Christ in his home (Matt. 18:20). In the absence of a father, the Lord himself steps in to fulfil the role (Psalm 68:5). In this sense, the Christian family is a church unit and believing parents, the logical and authorised choice to direct, guide and minister to their children.[2]

Making disciples

The traffic policeman gives orders from an elevated distance but is not required to know or relate at a personal level to those he directs. Parents, on the other hand, are meant to connect deeply with their kids – just as God the Father is in close relationship with the Son and Holy Spirit. Our parental authority, therefore needs to be embedded in relationship and fellowship with our child.

In his last instructions in Matthew 28:16-20, Jesus charged his followers, not only to tell people the Good News, but to make disciples. As Christians we are likely to be aware of many people around us who need to know Christ and be discipled. We are probably eager to get on with the job too! But as Christian parents, our children are first on the list of people we are to be discipling. We have seen many people raised in Christian families turn away from God when they are older often because, for whatever

---

1   See Deut. 11 (particularly v. 19); Prov. 22:6
2   Bill Banks, *Deliverance for children and teens* p.112

reason, their parents were unable to connect deeply with them to disciple them effectively.

The discipleship process prepares and enables us to relate to God independently later on. At a basic level, a disciple is someone who, through close contact, follows and imitates their leader. The disciples lived with Jesus at close quarters, twenty-four seven – for three years. They listened to and learned from his words and actions. Then they copied him. It didn't always turn out so well; but Jesus helped, encouraged and corrected them. It seems he never lost sight of what they would become. Even though they were a motley, rough-around-the-edges kind of bunch, they would end up spreading the Gospel throughout their known world, forever changing the course of mankind. How our children need this kind of close accompaniment from parents who see them as they are now and are committed to helping them become all they can be!

How Jesus did it

Seeing our children with the eyes of Christ, does not mean glossing over their faults. It means seeing who they are and who they will become in Christ, thus preparing them to fulfil their potential. Part of the discipleship process is dealing with things that are difficult, unpleasant or even threatening. Again, Jesus models this for us so perfectly!

Take the example of Peter, the hot-headed disciple, who chopped off a high-priest servant's ear in an attempt to stop his teacher being arrested. Then, having sworn only hours earlier to follow Jesus even unto death, Peter ends up denying him just as emphatically three times. The fact that Jesus had warned Peter that he would deny him, only makes Peter feel worse. Disappointed in himself and dejected, Peter went back to his old job as a fisherman and that would have been the end of the story – except that Jesus rose from the dead.

But for Peter, even that did not make any difference until he experienced Jesus in a special moment on the shores of lake Galilee. As they eat breakfast, Jesus takes Peter through a kind of inner healing experience. Jesus asks Peter three times if he loves him. Peter responds each time, that he loves – or at least likes – Jesus (John 21:15-17). Perhaps 'like' is all that Peter could bring himself to say after having abandoned Jesus in his hour of need. But, in one of the most tender passages in Scripture, Jesus entrusts this broken, humbled and disillusioned man with feeding his lambs and tending his sheep!

So, Jesus invested time and effort in teaching the disciples entrusted to him how to deal with things that could destroy them, such as hurts, sin and mistakes. He also taught them about Satan's kingdom, how it operates and how to defeat it at a personal and corporate level.[3] If we are entrusted with discipling children, then we need to know, model and teach them the things Christ taught his disciples. It should be routine for us to do so.

Relationship

Heart-to heart relationship is at the core of discipleship and the healing home. This kind of relationship doesn't happen by default, nor do you have an inherent right or access to your child's heart. It is relationship built purposefully over time. And it takes *quantity*, not just quality time to build the kind of relationship where a child will let you into their heart.

Children don't necessarily open up when it suits us. But you can position yourself to be on hand when they do and when it matters. You can spend as much time with them as possible, doing and being and making the effort to look them in the eyes and listen to what they are really communicating.

This heart-to-heart relationship will enable you to notice changes in your child, indications that they might be struggling. Your child will also be more likely to open up to you about what is troubling them than to someone else. You share a special bond and have unique access to their heart and they have seen you care in tangible ways. They feel safe with you. As they do so, you will be there to guide and teach them how to deal with situations and issues – God's way.

---

3   E.g. Matthew 4: 1-11; Matthew 16:19; Mark 5:1-20; Luke 8: 2; Matthew 12: 22-30

Make it a priority, therefore, to build and maintain a strong relationship with your child. Hugs and cuddles, play, story-telling, working side-by-side on tasks, listening attentively with eye-contact when they tell you something that is important to them are just some of the ways you can build a strong bond to your child from day one.

Finally, demonstrate unconditional love for them, the kind Jesus showed Peter. Unconditional love says, "I love you because of who you are, not because of what you do or fail to do. I love you no matter how you make me feel or look." Unconditional love is demonstrated by boundaries and consequences which aim, not to control and dominate, but to mould and build the godly character necessary for kids to truly thrive in every area of life now and in future.

Pause for thought

How would you describe your relationship with your child today? Is it more on the traffic policeman or the heart-to-heart discipleship side?

What practical step could you take towards building a deeper connection with your child? (see extras for more ideas)

7. Picking up signs and signals

Discerning what is really going on

The stronger the relationship with your child is, the easier it will be for you to pick up signs and signals that they may be struggling with an issue and need your help dealing with it. If you notice changes in their normal behaviour or sense they are just not thriving as they could be, take a closer look at what has happened or is happening in their life.

Possible signs of a problem include:

- Changes in normal behaviour e.g. aggression, withdrawal
- Sad, frightened or angry eyes
- Avoiding eye-contact
- Anti-social behaviour
- Evasive answers
- Confusion
- Retreat into fantasy world
- Acts out/draws unusually violent or sexual scenes

Pick up on what you see

Children, particularly the very young, live in the here and now. They need help in learning to process and cope with what comes their way each day. Spiteful words, like "everyone hates you!" can wound some children deeply. If a parent is on hand, an incident like this can be processed swiftly. But by the evening, a child may no longer be in the mood to talk about what happened in the morning. The chances are they will have *coped* with it in some way, but not necessarily processed and *dealt* with it. For this reason, if at all possible, we would encourage you to bring your child up yourself. Or at least try to be there when they leave for and get home from school. You may need to make certain sacrifices to be able to spend more time with your child. But it is well worth it!

Esther recalls:

"My mother would take one look at me when I came home from school and seemed to know immediately how I was. As a teenager, this sometimes annoyed me; but I was also grateful that she cared. Our daily routine included drinking a cup of tea together after school. Mum would listen attentively and ask questions about my day. Nothing was too trivial to be talked through. No problem was too big or small for God and us to handle together in prayer! If I had come home upset about something, talking to Mum encouraged me and I was soon able to face the world again – and my homework!

I was grateful to Mum for the security, warmth and comfort this daily routine gave me, particularly as a teen. So I have followed this pattern with our children, to this day. This enables me to pick up on what is going on in their hearts and lives. I have been on hand to teach them how to deal quickly with hurt or anger, to be quick to forgive, to set things right with others as soon as possible. I am so grateful for this privilege!"

Process versus cope

Developing a certain measure of resilience and thick skin is vital in developing a healthy personality. So we are not talking about smothering our kids or making them bare their souls and talk about absolutely everything with us. What is important is reading the signs and being there when they need help handling something. If children are *continually* left to deal with things on their own, they are likely to develop unhealthy coping strategies, such as denial, aggression, over-performance or substance and food abuse. How many adults are still relying on the same unhelpful coping strategies they developed as kids – and hurting themselves and others in the process?

Reacting to disclosure

"I am in *loco parentis*, your parent at school, you can turn to me for anything!" Kind words from a class teacher at the beginning of the 8th grade....

One lunch time, I (Esther) took the plunge and took that teacher at his word. I confided in him that the meanness and bullying of another member of staff was upsetting our whole class. We couldn't take it anymore; we needed his help. "You were right to confide in me," he said. " I will sort it out." Less than ten minutes later the teacher who had been harassing us stormed in, accused me of complaining about her behind her back. This reduced me to tears. "How could that teacher have done this to me?" I asked myself, silently shocked. It was the last time I confided in a teacher.

Perhaps you have had a similar experience? Perhaps you opened up to someone – only to have them laugh at you or belittle your worries or problems? You confided, only to be betrayed. If you have, I'll bet, like me, you never confided in that person again! You might even have vowed not to reveal weakness or to trust *anyone* again.

How we react to our children when they communicate with us – verbally and non-verbally – will determine the degree to which they will open up to us for help in future. We can't take it for granted that our child will open up to us about inner issues – just because we are their Mum or Dad. Children are incredibly perceptive and pick up on what we transmit. Such as whether we are really listening, or thinking more about the next phone call we need to make. They can sense if we basically find them a burden, consider their existence a mistake or are generally disappointed in them for some reason.

If they open up, they will expect you to listen and support at the very least and to take action in situations they cannot resolve on their own.

Pause for thought

How can you position yourself to pick up signals from your child better?

How do you deal with hurtful situations (coping strategies)? How do you think your child does?

8. Your Christian mind-set
Child-like trust and spirit-led watchfulness

We've talked about the importance of the parent-child relationship and your presence in the healing home. But how can we prepare our minds and spiritual climate in our home so that we can deal effectively with the needs and issues that come to the surface? We find a key to this by looking at how Jesus responded to the children that were brought to him when he was on earth; and what he had to say to the adults about faith and trust in that context.

The right address

God is serious about meeting children's needs and we need to be like them to receive from him. In Matthew 19 verse 13 we read:

"Then people brought little children to Jesus for him to place his hands on them and pray for them. But the disciples rebuked them."

Perhaps the disciples thought the children were a noisy disturbance or a distraction, from the 'real' business of teaching, healing and delivering adults. Did they think that it was beneath their Master's dignity to concern himself with small children? Or that the kids were too young to understand and cooperate enough to receive much from Jesus. However, Jesus stops the disciples in their tracks:

"Let the little children come to me, and do not hinder them, for the kingdom of heaven belongs to such as these" (Matthew 19:14).

He then goes on in the next verse to place his hands on them. Only when he has done so, does he move on: *"When he [Jesus] had placed his hands on them, he went on from there."*

Each child must have had some kind of emotional, physical or spiritual need, which is why the parents brought them and why Jesus laid hands on them. Can you imagine the love, blessing, joy, power, healing and freedom these children must have received?

So, if Jesus welcomed kids and met their needs while he was here on earth, without a shadow of doubt he wants to do that now from heaven. No matter what circumstances your child, or the child you care for, was conceived or is growing up in, no matter their behaviour or the issues they may be facing, God loves and welcomes them today. If you bring that child to Him, he will not turn them away!

A child-like heart releases God's power

Have you noticed how small children tend to trust their parents implicitly? Abuse, neglect or severe rejection from a parent breaks this instinctive trust, but otherwise, a child will look instinctively to a parent to meet their every need. They are the centre of that child's universe. In their eyes and experience, their parent knows everything, can do everything and anything!

This heart attitude of child-like faith and trust is what Jesus is getting at when he says, *the kingdom of heaven belongs to such as these.* We need this type of child-likeness as we bring our children to God!

Child-likeness is characterised by:

- Confidence – My heavenly Dad is the strongest Dad in the universe.
- Peace and security – I know who my heavenly Dad is and thus, who I am.
- Righteous living – I know the attitudes and behaviour that please him.
- Faith – Father God can do anything at all.

Keeping the right focus

One of the biggest challenges as Christian parents today is to maintain a child-like focus on God, particularly when experts of all shapes and sizes crowd in with advice.

When the disciples tried to keep the parents and their children from Jesus, it seems that they too had lost sight of who Jesus was and what he could do. As the crowds pressed in, they reverted to thinking in terms of the world's values and ways of doing things. How quickly this can happen to us too! We have seen Jesus and follow him. We know what he has done in our lives, but when problems arise, we revert to our old ways of thinking and rely on ourselves to find solutions! This attitude hinders the power of God from flowing in fullness into situations. Child-like trust, on the other hand, expects and believes that God wants to and will help. Always. Every time. Without fail.

Discern roots of problems

Just as our children turn instinctively to us, so we need to (re-)learn to turn intuitively to our Heavenly Father on behalf of our child. As we turn to God in child-like faith and trust expecting him to help, we allow his Spirit to show us what is going on inside our child and what they *really* need in a given situation.

Being led by the Spirit in this way has saved us a lot of worry, energy and resources over the years. So many times, as we brought a child to God in prayer, running through questions like those below in our minds, he showed us the root of a problem and subsequently the best way to help the child.

Questions to consider:

- Is the root of the issue physical, emotional or spiritual – or a mixture?
- Do they need medical attention?
- Do they just need to talk about something bothering them?
- Has my child been hurt by something someone did or said to them?
- Does my child need help putting things right with God and/or others?
- Are they under demonic influence or spiritual attack?
- Do they just need a drink, a hug or a good night's sleep?
- Do they need practical support or help in some way?

Let the King surprise you

Some issues are straightforward. The cause, or root, of the problem is clear. For example, if your child falls off a wall and breaks a leg, the remedy is obvious – a trip to the hospital to have it set.

But even in situations requiring natural solutions, cultivate the habit of turning to God and involving him from the start. How he loves to help and surprise us, as we experienced one hot summer with our youngest son:

When our youngest son was in the sixth grade, he broke his finger. A plaster cast all the way up to his elbow seemed a bit over the top to us, but there was no way around it. The hospital insisted he needed it and the cast meant no swimming. Peter was devastated. It was the start of the season, and he had been looking forward to cooling off in the lakes and rivers near our home in Zurich every day. Now he was destined to sit on the bank and watch his friends have fun – for three whole weeks. We brought him to Jesus in prayer, believing for a miracle. His leader at church also had faith and prayed for miraculous healing. When Peter went for a check up just six days later, they x-rayed his finger to make sure the bone was setting properly. To our delight, the doctor pronounced that there was no need to put the cast back on. He didn't need it anymore! Peter asked the doctor if it was normal for him to remove plaster casts after just six days, to which he replied, "no, I don't usually do this!" "So can I go swimming then?" Peter asked. "Yes, you can swim, but be careful with diving. Your finger is a little weak and you don't want to break it again!"

Go for it!

When Jesus was taken up into heaven, he sat down at the right hand of the Father (Mark 16:19). Why did he sit down? Because he had done what was necessary from his side and had already authorised his followers to carry on in his Name (Matt 28:18-20). Before he left Jesus said:

"Very truly I tell you, whoever believes in me will do the works I have been doing, and they will do even greater things than these, because I am going to the Father." (John 14:12)

Therefore, if Jesus placed his hands on children and met their needs, as his followers, we can do the same. If we have child-like faith and trust in God we can place our hands on our children and minister to them. No matter what their needs might be. No matter how big or small. We do this in the Name of Jesus Christ and using his authority. It is as if His hands are touching them, as his resurrection power flows through us to meet their needs. This is the heart of the healing home.

Pause for thought

How child-like is your faith and trust in God?

Talk to God about any issues your child struggles with. Thank God that he welcomes your child and is willing and able to help.

Imagine yourself placing your hands on your child in the Name of Jesus to meet their needs. If you are not used to praying for other people, using your imagination in this way can help you get used to the idea of doing so.

9. The importance of the big questions

Cultivating faith that is honest and supernatural

You can do everything in your power to cultivate an atmosphere of faith and trust in your home, but as soon as your child steps outside the front door, they are exposed to influences and experiences which can challenge their faith and raise big questions. We wanted to give our children the chance to develop the ability to own their faith – including the prayers and tools in this book – at an intellectual, practical and supernatural level. So we made it a priority to be in dialogue and prayer with our kids about what they saw and experienced both inside and outside the home. We knew that unresolved pain and unanswered questions have the potential to destabilise our inner world and shipwreck faith. Doubt and unbelief, if left to grow, can erode away faith and trust making it more difficult for children to receive all that God has for them.

So the question is how is your child going to process pain and painful experiences? How are you going to help them develop their own faith? What answers can you give them to big questions like: Why did this hurt happen? Why doesn't God try harder to make the world better? Why do Christians fail so often? How can I reconcile anti-Christian teaching from school with what I hear at home? Hasn't science disproved faith? What about faith versus religion? How can I find purpose and meaning in life? Whole books have been written on these questions and we can only offer brief answers to some of these questions here.[4]

Why doesn't God just make it better?

The following anecdote offers some parallels which may help you in answering some of these important questions.

---

4   If you need more info on these kind of topics, we recommend Derek Prince Ministries (derekprince. org) and Andrew Wommack Ministries (awmi.net).

One day, one of the pipes servicing our house in Argentina got blocked. Instead of clean water flowing in and dirty water out, the system jammed and sewage flooded into our back yard and front room. It was so horrible that the first plumber took one look at the situation and fled! It turned out that someone in the neighbourhood had flushed a pair of trousers down the toilet which got stuck because the pipes were so narrow and the plumbing system basic. In the same way, there can be blockages to the power of God flowing fully in our lives. Sometimes we need to find out exactly what these are and remove them using the corresponding prayers. Blockages can take many forms, including our own sins, the sins of others, demonic interference, ignorance and misunderstandings about who God is and what he wants for us.

One of the greatest gifts God has given us as human beings is the ability to choose and make decisions ourselves. Sometimes our choices hurt others. In the above story, someone made a careless, selfish choice not to dispose of old clothing properly – and we suffered as a result. To stop all the suffering and injustice in the world, God would constantly have to intervene and override people's choices. Doing so would effectively turn us into robots, incapable of meaningful relationship with him.

In addition to suffering arising from the consequences of human choice, the Bible shows that some suffering relates to the fallen state of creation. One day, God will make things perfect again and there will be no more suffering. In the meantime things can happen to us which he does not necessarily want for his world. People and pets die, natural disasters wipe out lives and spoil landscapes. And all we can do is mourn with those who mourn.

Finally, kids need to know that we have an active enemy. Satan tries everything he can to try to spoil our lives. He tries to throw "jeans" of all shapes and sizes into our systems. Instead of fresh water he wants us to experience smelly sewage. We look more at his role later in this chapter.

Key truths:

- God loves me and gave his life for me (Gal. 2:20)
- God is good and good things come from him (James 1:17)
- We can choose to do things which hurt ourselves and others (Gal. 5:13)
- One day God will make everything right and fair again (Rev. 21:4)
- If we love God, we can expect him to bring good out of the bad stuff that happens to us (Rom. 8:28)

Intellectual and practical questions

Two of our sons were taught the theory of evolution during dinosaur projects in primary school. Now we had taught them that God made the heavens and the earth, so what they heard at school raised questions like: "Does what the teacher says mean I can't believe in God and the Bible anymore?" Daniel took time to discuss and research these issues with the boys. As a result they grew intellectually and spiritually. Rather than being shipwrecked, they began to own their own faith in a Creator God of power.

We needn't be afraid of talking about doubts and tackling intellectual questions with our children. God can take it – and you can learn to take it too! If you don't know the answer to a question, just say: "That's a good question. You know what, I don't know the answer. But I'll try to find out. Let's talk about it again." Make sure you do look for answers and be sure to bring up the topic again as soon as possible.

Children also need to develop a faith that not only answers their intellectual and emotional questions, but is relevant to and works on a practical level in every area of life. Take time to talk to them about faith and science, life-style, entertainment, money, sexuality, politics, etc. Teach them God's heart and values and how you apply these to each area of life. Help them discover their gifts and purpose in life by giving them opportunities to try new things and find an occupation where they can use their talents.

Faith versus religion

Some church systems foster religion, doubt and fear. For example, a friend of one of our sons was very interested in Jesus, but had been told at his church that the Bible was full of contradictions. He knew we believed in the Bible and asked us what we thought. We had a good discussion about why we believe the Bible is reliable and how it helps us live a full life today.

Make every effort to be part of a Bible-preaching, spirit-filled, faith-building church, whatever denomination that may look like where you live. But even if you are in such a church, remember, your child may still need help processing what they hear and see because no church is perfect! Be vigilant, not controlling. Talk to your children about what they learn at children's church or at youth group. Remember, as parents we, not the pastor or kids leader, are ultimately responsible for our child's spiritual instruction.

The importance of the supernatural

Children generally have less trouble than adults believing in and praying for miracles. They can often see into the spiritual realm as a matter of course. When our youngest son was five, Esther was sitting on his bed chatting one night, when he reported, in a matter-of-fact way, that he had recently seen an angel fly across his room. He said it made him feel good to think that God was watching over him in this way. We believe that he had seen into the spiritual realm and literally seen an angel at a time when he particularly needed to feel God's care.

When the unseen world and the supernatural dimensions of the Kingdom of heaven (e.g. miracles) are denied or explained away, children can become interested in the occult instead. The reason for this is that the paranormal appeals to the spiritual dimension of their being. But the occult exposes them to the unseen demonic world.[5]

Explain to your child that, in addition to the world we can see, there is a world they cannot see. An unseen spiritual realm. This is made up of the

---

5   See section E for more info.

kingdom of light, where God is honoured and obeyed and the kingdom of darkness, where Satan is obeyed. These two kingdoms are in conflict with each other – even today. A battle is raging although the outcome is already known. God wins! Satan and his demons have *already* been defeated through the cross of Christ (Col. 2:15); but they work hard to deceive people and to entice them into working evil and destruction (Rev. 12:9).

Children need at least a basic understanding of this spiritual background to deal with both natural questions and demonic attacks on their faith. They also need to understand and know that they are children of God with amazing power and authority they can use to defeat the enemy in their lives and do the works of Christ (Eph. 1:19-20).

As your children experience victory and God's supernatural power working in and through them, their faith and trust will grow. We saw this when our son, Samuel, was eleven. His groin injury was miraculously healed at a meeting for kids at a friend's house. He said later that night: "I sometimes wondered, if God really existed. But now I know he does, because I experienced his power in my own body. He healed me. I couldn't raise my leg properly before and now I can!"

Pause for thought

Do you think your child might have doubts or difficulty trusting God?

What influences, events or people might have shaken their faith and trust in Him?

10. Creating a healing home
Steps to embracing your role and setting the tone

The healing home is a place where each family member feels loved, valued and safe sharing a problem, showing weakness and making mistakes. It may take time and effort to change the atmosphere and relationships in your home – but it is never too late to start. Here, are ten steps to help you move in the right direction.

1. Adopt a Christ-centred culture

A 'family culture' is the sum of the beliefs and attitudes, behaviours and past experiences that each parent brings into the home. As Christians, the culture of our home needs to be submitted to and transformed by biblical values, instruction and truth. When this happens, we align ourselves with the mission of Christ (Luke 4:18) and our home becomes a place of healing, freedom and transformation.

2. Let God work in you

We were both fully committed to creating a healing home, because healing and freedom prayers had revolutionised our own lives. 2 Corinthians 1:4 says that we can comfort others with the comfort we have received. In other words, we can't pass on to our kids what we have not received from God ourselves. Many parents struggle to comfort their own kids because of the pain in their own heart.

Consider:

- Have I received God's comfort in my life?
- Am I secure in God's love for me? Do I love myself?
- Do I allow myself to have problems and make mistakes?

We talked about taking an honest look at your own life and allowing God to show you any areas of your life which still need his healing touch or correction in the previous section. As God works in your life, your capacity to meet your child's needs effectively increases. As you grow in confidence and authority you will be able to discern and resist the attacks of the evil one on your child's life, as well.

3. Embrace parenthood

If you focus on parenting (skills and processes involved in supporting development) rather than on parenthood (the state of being a parent), you will feel insecure. For example, if you are focused on parenting and you see your child has a problem, you will strive to find the right method or strategy. But if your starting point is parenthood, you will be confident that the solutions will emerge from your relationship with God and your child.

We can embrace parenthood because it is God's idea, not ours. He is the ultimate heavenly Father. Understanding the father heart of God is fundamental to both your own relationship with God and your relationship with your child. Your unique parent-child relationship was born in the heart of God and your child needs a relationship with *you*. After all, who else is positioned to know them so entirely, love them unconditionally and watch their back selflessly? Methods and strategies won't cut it.

4. Set priorities and stay focused

How many kids today are juggled around to fit in with adult lives? How many more feel like a dropped ball, struggling to make sense of the world and life, wondering if anyone notices, or even cares, about the pain inside? If you don't guide and support your child, they are likely to look elsewhere – or nowhere. If your teen is not talking to you, they might not actually be talking to anyone. And that is a very lonely place to be.[6] A Swiss sixteen-year old said:

"Several of my friends are struggling with big issues, like parental divorce and depression, but we rarely get beyond superficial talk with each other. None of us want to lose face or show weakness. If you did, you'd never live

---

6   Dr. Gordon Neufeld makes this point based on his extensive experience as developmental psychologist. For more on this, see his book, *Hold onto your kids: Why parents need to matter more than peers.*

it down. It's safer just to keep up appearances and post holiday snap shots and stuff like that on Instagram."

So, keep focused and order your priorities regularly. Beware of things that take you away from your children particularly at critical times; be it work, a ministry, other people or things. Make and keep your kids your top priority – even if it means changing jobs, churches or just giving up a project or interest to be at home more.

5. Prize quantity time

Quality time is not the same as quantity time, no matter what people may say. Just being around can mean more than you think. Wherever possible, choose less of other things and more quantity time with your kids.

A child can usually tell the difference between a parent who can't and a parent who won't make more time for them. If you currently have no choice but to rely on quality rather than quantity time, then tell your child that you would want to be around more if it were possible. Tell them you think about them and pray for them throughout the day.

6. Prioritise communication

Creating opportunities to communicate effectively with your child in today's busy world takes skill and determination. But good communication, verbal and non-verbal, is key to the healing home. How else can we hope to pick up on what a child is 'saying' or communicate with them? This is such a crucial step to building a healing home that we have included ideas on how to improve communication opportunities in the home in the Extras.

7. Face issues

We all get hurt and face challenges. We sin and are targets for demonic attack. The sooner we face this reality, the quicker we can learn God's way of dealing with things. As the healing and freedom culture in your home grows, issues will come to the surface. This makes many people uncomfortable and it can be scary, but facing up to truth is the first step to healing and freedom. Place your hand in God's hand and trust him to help you deal boldly and honestly with issues.

Similarly, disagreement and conflict are part of life. No family agrees on everything. But children need to know that their voice is heard and their opinion valued – even if they don't always understand your decisions or get their own way. Keep the lines of communication open and respectful. It can take time, patience and strong nerves to talk something through with a child until you reach a place of peace with each other again, but it is worth it.

8. Create a safe haven

Most big churches have a small group system because people can get lost in a crowd. The family is the ultimate small group. As leader of your family, your job is to create a safe space for your child to flourish and grow spiritually.

A safe haven enables children to:

- Hear, read and discuss God's Word openly
- Be still before the Lord in times of quiet and reflection
- Share what the Lord is doing in their life
- Talk about how God is using them to help others
- Talk about any difficulties or problems they may be struggling with
- Pray for each other for healing and freedom
- Intercede for others outside the group

Suggested ground rules:

- No situation is too small or silly to talk about if someone wants to
- We listen carefully when someone else is talking
- We keep what we have heard in the group to ourselves

9. Get into the freedom and healing way

Children may come home burdened by what they have seen, heard or experienced. For example, nastiness at school, a fight with a friend, an exam that went wrong, an accident they saw on the way home. Or they might simply be generally unhappy and lonely. Make a habit of helping children deal with issues as they share them with you, using the healing and freedom prayers in subsequent sections. You can do this informally, over a snack after school or by setting time aside to talk and pray at a deeper level.

Explain to your child that God is interested in our daily lives, our burdens and sorrows. Encourage them to bring things that bother them to God straight away. As your child experiences God meeting and touching them personally in everyday situations, their own relationship with the Lord will be strengthened. Eventually, dealing with issues with God's help will become second nature to them.

10. Create space for deep-level healing

Take signals that your child may be struggling with deeper issues seriously. Trust your gut instinct and overall impression. Make sure your child knows that you care and that they can turn to you for help. Create space to find out what is bothering them and assure them that you love them – no matter what is going on.

Issues can take time to pray and work through. Set aside a regular time (diary appointment) for this. Keep the appointment with your child with the same commitment you would a work engagement. Once you have identified the root of issues, use the healing and freedom prayers to deal with them. Keep supporting them in this way, until they have overcome the issue and been able to move forward.

Pause for thought

What kind of home atmosphere did you grow up in?

In what ways is your home already a healing home? Which step could you focus on today in working to establish a healing culture in your family?

11. The power of God's Word

Using Bible and God stories to overcome issues

Our parents loved God's Word and based their lives and actions on its teachings. As children we saw our parents reading and studying the Bible for themselves. We talked about it at home together. It was a living and active component of our home life as kids.

We also both learned Bible verses by heart from an early age. We found these verses would pop into our heads just when we needed them! This created further expectancy and momentum in our own Bible reading and prayer life as we grew older.

Whether you know God's Word well already or are just one step ahead of your child, don't miss out on teaching and helping them memorise God's Word. You will be laying an indescribably rich foundation in their life!

God's Word has power to heal and deliver

What is so special about the Bible? Won't any story book do? Unlike other literary genres, the Bible is "God-breathed" and contains eternal truths that speak and minister into the individual needs of hearers through the generations, across cultures (2 Tim. 3:16).

Far from being dry or outdated, it is fresh and relevant for kids. Our eldest son was fifteen when he put it this way: "The Bible is amazing. There is always something new to discover in a story – even in the ones I've heard so many times before. No other book is like that. It's so cool!"

The power of God's Word to touch children cannot be underestimated. Children need to hear and make room for it to work in their hearts. This is an important part of preparing children to be healed and set free.

The Bible is: *"...alive and active. Sharper than any double-edged sword, it penetrates even to dividing soul and spirit, joints and marrow...."* (Hebrews 4:12)

Similarly, God promises it will have an effect:

"...so is my word that goes out from my mouth: It will not return to me empty, but will accomplish what I desire and achieve the purpose for which I sent it." (Isaiah 55:11)

Bible stories

The men and women in the Bible are like us in so many ways! They might have worn different clothes and spoken another language, but they struggled with similar things – they got hurt, committed sins and came under demonic attack. They were lonely, fearful, rebellious and battled negative reactions, like jealousy and hatred. Some overcame issues, and are examples to us, others didn't and are warnings. Most children love stories, so Bible stories are a great way to help your child access and deal with similar issues in their own lives.

There are many creative and fun ways of helping your child get to know and love God's Word. Apart from a wealth of illustrated Bibles for all ages, there are apps, devotionals, Bible cartoons and films as well. And why not draw, model and photograph your favourite Bible stories together! The table below provides some suggestions of Bible stories that you can focus on for specific issues.

God stories

When God does something, share it with the others in the family. It could be anything, from finding a lost key after praying, to a headache going away after a simple prayer, to a verified miracle you hear about from other Christians. Get into the habit of sharing these God stories with each other regularly at bed or meal times. Doing so will create an atmosphere of faith in your home, and an expectancy that the God of the Bible can and wants to do miracles in your own lives and the lives of those around you!

Bible stories focusing on common issues:

Story	Scripture	Issue	Truth
David & Goliath	1 Samuel 17:1-52	Fear	God helps me defeat giants of fear in my life.
David and Mephibosheth	2 Samuel 9:1-12	Rejection	God loves and accepts me. I can be with him always.
Zacchaeus	Luke 19:1-10	Restitution	Jesus forgives me and helps me put things right.
Ruth	Ruth 1-4	Rootlessness; loss	I can belong to the people of God. With God's help I can be happy again.
Gideon	Judges 6 -7 (especially 6:12, 15-16)	Inferiority; domination; power of negative words	God sees me. I am a mighty warrior.
Joseph	Genesis 37, 39-47:12	Dysfunctional family background; traumatic events.	God has His hand over my life. He is with me to work everything together for good.
Saul	1 Samuel 13:1-15; 15: 1-34	Rebellion	God wants me to obey Him in my heart and actions.
Esther	Esther 1-10	Destiny; intimidation	God has a purpose for my life and gives me courage in every situation.
Jesus Christ	John 19	Abuse, mistreatment; false accusation, betrayal	Jesus was abused and mistreated. He suffered and understands my pain. He took it on Himself on the cross so I can be free and healed.
The unforgiving servant	Matthew 18:23-35	Forgiveness	I forgive others, just as God has forgiven me.
Peter	John 18:15-18, 25-27; 21:15-19	Failure; shame	I can come to Jesus when I fail. He takes away my guilt and shame. He uses me to help others.

Fictional and biographical stories

Sharing a story together is something many parents and kids enjoy. Why not include stories that are relevant to your child's situation as a springboard to talk and pray with them about what they are facing.

Older children love true stories that expand their geographical and historical horizons. Here are just three well known examples:

As a child, **Amy Carmichael** (1867-1951) hated her brown eyes and asked God to make them blue. She was disappointed when he didn't answer her prayers! Later, as a missionary in India, she soon realised that her brown eyes helped her blend in locally. God had created her perfect for the job he had in mind for her.

After her family was discovered hiding Jews in the Second World War, **Corrie Ten Boom** (1892-1983) was sent to a concentration camp. She survived unspeakable cruelty, but her sister died. Unexpectedly, years later, she came face to face with one of her captors and was able to forgive him.

Eric Liddell (1902-1945) qualified for the Paris Olympics only to find his best race, the 100m sprint, was set for a Sunday. He refused to run on the Lord's day and came under great pressure and ridicule. Holding fast to his convictions, he switched to 400m instead. To everyone's amazement he won the gold medal!

Pause for thought

How well do you know God's Word? Do you make time to read and study it daily?

Which Bible story could help your child overcome an issue they struggle with?

Is there a biographical or God story that could also help them in that area?

Tools for emotional healing

C.

TOOLS FOR EMOTIONAL HEALING

12. Empowering children to deal with hurts

Dealing with hurts now avoids problems later

No matter how hard you try to protect your child, they will get hurt. At some point. By someone or something. Because even the most dedicated parent can't be there all the time. The good news is that, while you cannot always protect your child from hurt, nor can you suffer in their place, there is something you can do. You can teach them to deal effectively with hurts – both great and small – by connecting them to someone who can. His name is Jesus Christ, the Saviour of the world.

The Bible tells us that this Jesus bore our sickness and hurts and that by his wounds we are healed (Isaiah 53:4-5). God knew you wouldn't be able to take every bullet for your child, nor suffer in their place – so he did it for you. He took every pain and carried every sorrow your child would ever face when he hung on the cross. His death and resurrection mean that they do not need to live with the hurts, nor bear the consequences of them for the rest of their lives. Their pain can be exchanged at the cross for peace, comfort and wholeness.

Treat emotional wounds and avoid infection

Hurts are like wounds that need to be treated to heal properly; even a seemingly trivial cut can end up presenting complications if infection sets in. That's why we disinfect and monitor our children's cuts and scrapes.

In the same way, emotional wounds require spiritual cleansing and dressing to heal well. If left untreated they can become spiritually infected, for example by damaging reactions like unforgiveness, bitterness and rejection. If nurtured, these emotions give way to unhelpful thought patterns and demonic strongholds, which in turn fuel destructive choices and behaviour.

An example of dealing with everyday hurts

Seven-year-old Noah, comes home from primary school one day. He seems quieter than usual, a little sad even. His mother gives him a drink. She can see that something is not quite right, so she asks him about his day and how his best friend, Joe is. She is surprised to find that he now hates Joe.

"Why do you hate him?" she asks.

"He laughed at me. He says I have big feet and big ears. And everyone else thinks so too."

"How do you know everyone thinks that?" his mother asks.

"Because everyone was laughing at me as well."

Noah starts to cry. His mother takes him in her arms and comforts him. When Noah stops crying, his mother looks him in the eye and says:

"You know, no matter what anyone else might think about you or your feet or ears or anything else about you, I like you the way you are. I love you! And you know what, God does too! Children are all different; some are tall, others small, some can run fast, others can't, some kids find maths easy, others find it really hard... Everyone has something about them that someone else could laugh at if they wanted to. People can be unkind – even best friends. When they are, it's horrible and really hurts. But God knows how it feels when people are unkind to us. Because they said horrible things to Jesus too. Even his best friends ran away from him! Now, how about we talk to Jesus about what Joe and these other kids said to you?"[1]

Notice that Noah's mother didn't minimise his feelings by encouraging him to simply brush it off. Neither did she tell him to toughen up. And she certainly didn't ignore it. Just as she would have made the effort to carefully disinfect a scraped knee, so Noah's mum knew that even an emotional surface wound is worth treating swiftly. So she took the time to talk and offered to pray with him about his day.

---

1   This example continues on at the end of the next chapter.

Dealing with hurts now – even simple ones – avoids problems later. For Noah, this could have taken one or more of the following forms:

- Self-rejection: "Everyone hates me. There must be something really wrong with me. I hate myself!"
- Aggression: "If everyone hates me, then I'll give them something to really hate."
- Withdrawal: "If even my best friend laughs at me, I'm best off on my own. Who needs friends anyway?!"

Can it really be that simple?

Can dealing with hurts really be as simple as talking with a child about a hurtful situation over a snack, and inviting them to bring their hurt to Jesus in prayer? The answer in our experience is yes, it can! But if a hurt goes deeper, or turns out to be older and spiritually infected already, you may need to treat it using a combination of the healing and freedom prayers as part of a healing process which can take time.

Whatever is required, remember that by helping a child deal with hurts, you are teaching them an *empowering lifestyle;* one which will help them avoid the pain and heartache spiritually-infected emotional wounds can cause in the future.

Pause for thought

How familiar are you with the idea that emotional hurts need treatment to avoid spiritual infection?

Thank Jesus Christ that he has taken your child's hurt and pain on the cross and by his wounds your child is healed (Isaiah 53:4-5).

13. How to forgive and deal with hurts

The hurts prayers

Many inner hurts in children can be healed in three simple steps. The hurts prayers work because they are rooted in eternal truth. You could actually just pray the three prayers given in the box below in faith with your child and the Lord would hear you and touch your child. In this chapter, we explain each of the steps in some depth. This will give you confidence to lead your child through these prayers, even as they grow older and start asking harder questions.

As you use these prayers, rely on the guidance and leading of the Holy Spirit. He is with you and will work through you to heal your child. Remember to adjust the vocabulary and specifics to suit your child's age and circumstances.

THE HURTS PRAYERS

1. Tell Jesus what is hurting you or why you feel sad inside.

2. Ask Jesus to heal your pain and make it better.
    (Put your hand on your heart as you do this).

3. Forgive the person who has hurt you.
    (Clench your fist. Then as you open it say, "I forgive you").

You can say ...

1. "**Hey Jesus**! I feel hurt because ..."

2. "**Please** Lord Jesus heal my heart."

3. "**I forgive** ... for what they did /what they said to me."

Thank you Jesus for healing my hurt!

Step 1. Tell the Lord Jesus what is hurting you or why you feel sad inside.

It is important that children are allowed to express their true feelings when hurt. You can tell them that the most famous songwriter in history was a king called David, who was very good at telling God when he got hurt and offended and disappointed.[2] He'd get things off his chest and then ask God to help, comfort and protect him and then thanked him for being a good God.

Now before David became king, he sang his songs and did other jobs around the palace for another king called Saul. But Saul was not interested in being best friends with God like David was. He was more interested in being King and having everyone like him. So he didn't talk to God much himself, though sometimes he asked others, like the prophets, to talk to God for him. When people began to like David more, Saul felt very bad. But he didn't tell God how jealous and hurt he felt, nor did he ask for his help. He just kept it all inside and got more and more angry. In fact he got so angry he couldn't think straight anymore and even tried to kill David.

Step 2. Ask the Lord Jesus to heal your pain and make it better.

Explain to your child that Jesus has been hurt as well. He was rejected and looked down upon and laughed at by other people. And that made him sad and hurt inside. Then he was hurt physically when they beat him up and finally he was killed on a cross. The Bible says that it is because Jesus was hurt that he can bring us healing:

"He was despised and rejected by mankind...Surely he took up our pain and bore our suffering...and by his wounds we are healed." (Isaiah 53:3-5)

Some children may find it helpful to imagine themselves sitting on Jesus' knee or standing next to him and simply saying, "Please Lord Jesus Christ, you were hurt by other people. You have carried my pain on the cross. I now give you my pain. Please heal my pain."

---

2   We can read the lyrics for many of his songs in the book of Psalms in the Bible.

Sometimes children feel an actual physical pain in their heart as they pray. This is the emotional pain coming up. They can put their hand where it is hurting and say, "Please Jesus Christ, take away my pain." Be careful not to rush them, but allow time for Christ to heal.

Step 3. Forgive those who hurt you.

In our experience, young children are often quick and eager to forgive, while older children may have more difficulty forgiving. In this case, you can bring up the Lord's Prayer – forgive us our sins as we forgive those who sin against us. Explain that forgiving frees us from the desire for revenge that always makes things worse.

Read the parable of the unforgiving servant in Matthew 18:21–32 together. The King represents God. The unforgiving servant stands for the person who won't forgive others. Expect God to speak to your child as you think about: The staggering amount of debt the King cancelled, the small debt his fellow servant owed him. You might also ask the question of what prison means?

All unforgiveness cuts us off from God. When we refuse to forgive, we place ourselves in a prison of our own making. There, we are tortured by negative emotions, lack of peace and demonic powers. If we want to be free, we need God's mercy. We will never be able to pay our debt off ourselves, that is clear. Forgiveness is the only way to end this prison sentence.

Remember that understanding the problem is an important part of forgiveness. Don't push a child into saying *"I forgive."* Some children need help in understanding that what was done to them was wrong. They might also need to understand how much God has forgiven them for their sins.[3]

Remember that Jesus said forgive seventy times seven (Matt. 18:22). That could be because people hurt us often, or because even after we say we forgive, negative thoughts and feelings about someone can still come back.

---

3   We look at sin and forgiveness in more detail in section D

Lastly, children sometimes ask whether they need to actually go and tell someone that they forgive them. In some situations, talking through a hurtful situation with the person who has hurt you and expressing that you forgive them could be helpful. For example, if friends have fought at school. However, there are many situations where confrontation is neither possible nor wise. A child may be too vulnerable to cope with the other person's reaction, and expressing forgiveness could be misunderstood and make matters worse. This is particularly true in cases where a parent has hurt a child. Or where a child has been abused. Your priority is to keep your child safe so they can heal – not expose them to further hurt.

A practical way to let go of hurt

Use this simple exercise to bring this step to life and help a child forgive. Find a heavy stone and let your child hold it in their closed fist.

Adult says: "Can you feel how heavy this stone is? Imagine if you had to hold this stone all day long. Your hands wouldn't be free to pick up any other toys and would get very sore! Holding onto hurt is like holding onto a stone. We are not free to receive God's forgiveness and all the other good things he wants to give us."

How about you let go of the stone and as you drop it, say "I forgive ..." (name the person who has hurt the child).

Child prays: "I forgive...(name of person) for what they did to me...(say what it is)."

Help your child to dispose of the stone safely.

Noah, (7) prays the hurts prayers

We met Noah in the previous chapter. His mum had noticed something was wrong and chatted to him about his day over tea. He had shared that he was hurting inside because his best friend, Joe and other children at school had laughed at him and said he had big feet and ears. We left them about to pray together. Here, is an example of what it might look like for

Noah's mum to use the hurts prayers in that situation to help him bring his pain to Jesus and forgive Joe and the other kids if that is what Noah wanted.

Mum: Would you like to tell Jesus what happened at school today and how you feel?

Noah: Hey Jesus! I feel bad. I feel like everyone hates me. Everyone was horrible to me at school today. Even Joe. I thought he was my best friend....

Mum: Can you bring the pain to Jesus? How about putting your hand on your heart and asking Jesus to heal the pain and take it away?

Noah: Please Lord Jesus, heal my hurt and take this pain away.

Mum: Can you forgive Joe and the other kids for being horrible to you and laughing at you?

Noah: Yes I can. I forgive Joe and all the other kids for being horrible to me and laughing at me.

Mum: How do you feel now?

14. Breaking the power of negative reactions

Hurt children hurt children

We have seen how children can bring their hurts to Jesus using the hurts prayers. But this is really only the first part of healing hurts effectively. The next stage is dealing with our own reactions to what was said or done to us which all too often can hurt ourselves and others. For example, we may say spiteful things to get our own back, or start to ignore and hate someone we thought was a friend, or turn on ourselves and decide we must be stupid and unlovable to have been treated that way in the first place.

While we may be able to understand and even justify these kind of reactions to hurt at some human level, holding onto them actually causes us more problems. Dealing with our reactions towards situations and people who have hurt us, on the other hand, is like putting disinfectant on a wound. It kills off any bacteria and enables the wound to heal properly.

Tom (8)

When Tom's mother came to see us she was at her wits end. Her eight-year- old son had become aggressive at school and prone to rages at home. From where he lay wedged half-way under our coffee table, Tom began to open up about how angry he felt that his best friend had turned against him. He wanted to make him suffer!

We explained to Tom, that Jesus knew how he felt, because he had been abandoned by his close friends, the disciples, too. But that Jesus told us to forgive our enemies and those who wrong us. We also explained that this anger was fuelling his aggression. But he – not his friend – was the one getting into all the trouble at school! So a smart thing to do would be to follow Jesus' instructions, forgive the boy and ask forgiveness for his own anger and let go of it.

Tom decided to do this, forgave the other boy and gave his hurt and anger about him to Jesus. He asked God to forgive him for hurting others, including his mum, by his own aggressive behaviour in response to feeling hurt.

Assuming responsibility for our reactions

Many people never get beyond what was done to them. They get stuck in a victim mentality and may unwittingly encourage others, like their kids, to adopt the same attitude. But this is not doing anyone any favours. If we want to deal with hurts thoroughly and move forward, we need to face and deal with our reactions – God's way.

Many of the negative reactions to hurts one could think of can be found listed under what the Bible calls 'works of the flesh'. God doesn't like them because they go against his character and are therefore sinful (Galatians 5:19). They spoil our lives and give the devil a foothold. God expects us to take full responsibility for our reactions and resulting actions and to deal with them accordingly:

- *"Get rid of all bitterness, rage and anger, brawling and slander, along with every form of malice. Be kind and compassionate to one another, forgiving each other, just as in Christ God forgave you."* (Ephesians 4:31-32)
- *"In your anger do not sin: Do not let the sun go down while you are still angry, and do not give the devil a foothold."* (Ephesians 4:26-27)

Avoiding chain reactions

Negative reactions can set off a whole chain of other negative reactions inside us. But if we deal with our reactions this can be largely avoided. Consider the following example:

Imagine fifteen-year-old Vanessa sitting alone in her room. She can't believe it's over. She's been dumped. By SMS. He couldn't even be bothered to tell her to her face! She can't believe the humiliation – not to mention how much it just plain hurts. She really liked the guy. He was the one. But he didn't want her anymore!

As the days go by, Vanessa begins to think more and more that something must be basically wrong with her. "I'm fat and ugly" she concludes. "If I was as slim as Jessica, then Ethan would still want me!" Vanessa starts skipping meals and jogging before school. She begins to lose weight and feels better about herself. But she's not satisfied, she needs to be smaller! As her identity and self-worth become increasingly bound up with how she looks, Vanessa find it increasingly difficult to love and accept herself – and maintain healthy eating habits.

Imagine, however, if instead of spiralling down into pain and self-hatred, Vanessa is shown how to bring her feelings of self-rejection to the Lord and receive his comfort. She asks God to forgive her for starting to reject herself and her body. She hears the Lord whisper words of love to her through Scriptures, such as: "I am fearfully and wonderfully made" (Psalm 139:14a). She realises Ethan's rejection of her has nothing to do with her fundamental worth. Dealing with her reactions may not bring her boy-friend back, but it will help her heal properly and develop a self-esteem. One which is based on God's love for her and not how others treat her, all of which are essential foundations for a happy marriage in the future.

When reactions are suppressed

An Argentine teenager, Esteban, had backache and unaccountable pains in his body. At one point, he described to Daniel how his father had pun-ished him when he was a child by pouring boiling water over him. He felt no emotion as he related this incident, but he did say that he thought he must have done something to deserve the punishment. It took a long time for Esteban to understand that no matter what he or any child might have done, *nothing* could ever justify such a punishment. When he finally understood this he was ready to deal, not only with the trauma itself, but also with his suppressed reactions of hatred towards his father. When he had done this, he was set free from the pain in his body!

Esteban is an example of how kids will find different ways to cope with hurt. Sometimes it takes time to get passed these coping strategies to heal the hurts and deal with suppressed reactions. You may have developed a few coping strategies of your own depending on your upbringing. And your kids may have copied yours or developed some of their own.

Common coping strategies include:

- **Fight:** I'll get my own back. I'm going to make them pay.
- **Protect:** No-one is ever going to get close and hurt me like that again.
- **Deny:** It wasn't really that bad, I'm fine. Other people suffer worse.
- **Ignore:** I don't want to talk about it. It's not important. Let's move on.
- **Bury:** I'll deal with it later.
- **Excuse:** He couldn't help it. He didn't know any better. He was sick.
- **Justify:** I can't help my reactions. I'm the victim here!

All these sorts of strategies hinder effective emotional healing, which is essential to moving beyond hurts to flourish.

Pause for thought

Do any of the coping strategies listed describe the way you or your child deal with hurt?

How does what the Bible has to say about the 'works of the flesh' help break the power of negative reactions in your life?

15. Learning to respond better

The reactions prayers

We have seen how important it is to teach children to deal, not only with their own hurt, but with the negative reactions those hurts produce in their own lives. These reactions can take the form of feelings, thoughts, words or actions, which can result in hurt children hurting themselves and others. Help your child break the power of negative reactions in their lives using these easy-to-grasp prayer steps.

Once again, you can just use the steps listed below, but the rest of the chapter will equip you with the biblical understanding that will help you to raise your child in understanding.

THE REACTIONS PRAYERS

1. Tell Jesus how you feel about what happened.
   Tell him if you said or did something wrong because you were hurt.

2. Ask Jesus to forgive you for holding on to these feelings.
   Say sorry for doing or saying wrong things.

3. Ask Jesus to take away the bad feelings related to the hurt.

You can say ...

1. **"Hey Jesus!** I feel... inside because of ... I did/I said... because I was hurt."

2. **"Please** forgive me Jesus for holding on to these feelings and for doing or saying wrong things."

3. **"I ask** you to take away this feeling of..."

Thank you Jesus for forgiving me and taking these feelings away!

Step 1. Tell Jesus how you feel about what happened. Tell him if you said or did something wrong because you were hurt.

Teaching children to honestly express their reactions to hurt is important and valid. Psalm 62:8 says: *"Trust in him at all times, you people; pour out your hearts to him, for God is our refuge."* Talking to God about our reactions to hurt is not about indulging negative feelings or dwelling on hurt, which encourages a victim mentality. Rather, by telling God how we feel in an attitude of trust, we position ourselves to receive his help in dealing with what can sometimes be difficult and overwhelming reactions to hurts. In fact some reactions can be so powerful that, unless he helps us deal with them, we can end up hurting ourselves and others as a result.

Part of expressing reactions to hurts includes sorting out facts like, what exactly happened, who did or said what to whom, which reactions are helpful and which unhelpful? This prepares the child to take the next step. With that in mind, we look briefly at three common reactions to hurts – rejection, anger and fear.

Rejection

One of the most common hurts that people of all ages can experience is rejection. It makes us feel so bad inside that keeping these feelings, can set a child off on one of two potentially destructive paths. [4]

Outward destruction: *Rejection > Rebellion > Resentment > Bitterness > Hatred > Anger > Rage > Violence > Murder*

Inward destruction: *Rejection > Self-pity > Withdrawal > Depression > Hopelessness > Suicide*

A child can react with a mixture of both rebellion and self-pity. But a much better response is to learn, from a young age, to bring these reactions to Jesus, ask his forgiveness where we have hurt others as a result of keeping these feelings and ask him to take them away.

---

4   A and E Taylor, *Ministering Below the Surface* Section 4 Key Teachings, Rejection, First Edition, p. 118

Anger

Anger is a common reaction to hurt and merits special consideration. Some people have the idea that a good Christian never gets angry. They sweep any feelings of anger under the carpet and end up putting up with all sorts of injustice as a result. They teach their kids to "turn the other cheek" in situations where they would actually need help defending themselves. Others let off steam and hurt people claiming they have a right to be angry or just need to get things off their chest.

But the Bible says *"in your anger, do not sin"* (Eph. 4:26). What does this mean when it comes to helping kids deal with anger as an understandable reaction to hurt? Imagine for a moment the teen in an Argentine shanty town who is beaten for no reason other than he happened to be home when his drunken father showed up. He is likely to have a lot of (justifiable) anger towards his father. Rather than repenting of anger, however, this teen would need help to hand his anger over to God. Holding on to it could lead him to sins such as: Swearing vengeance on his father (Rom. 12:19), judging him (Matt. 7:1) or becoming bitter (Heb. 12:15). If this boy has already gone down these paths, then he would need to ask God's forgiveness for those reactions; but not for feeling angry or indignant that he was beaten for no reason.

Step 2. Ask Jesus to forgive you for holding on to these feelings. Say sorry for doing or saying wrong things.

Hurt children hurt children as we have seen. In this process the victim often becomes a perpetrator. This needs to be dealt with in prayer. Simply say sorry for what we have done, said, felt or thought as a result of being hurt and ask the Lord Jesus to forgive us. By confessing negative reactions and asking God to forgive us, we align ourselves with Christ and choose to follow his example. Though falsely accused, beaten and killed, Jesus responded with forgiveness and love for his enemies. Teaching children to assume their part in reacting to hurt in no way minimises the hurt or excuses what was done to them. Neither is it saying that they should not learn to stand their ground and stand up for themselves in the playground. Boys particularly need to know that it is all right to do so. But it does protect a child's heart from bitter roots, from developing a debilitating victim mentality and allows God to fully heal their hurts so they can truly move on.

Remember, it is important that a child knows, that if he or she has asked for forgiveness, then God has indeed forgiven them. They have that promise in 1 John 1:9:

"If we confess our sins, he is faithful and just and will forgive us our sins and purify us from all unrighteousness."

We look at forgiveness of sins in more detail in section D.

Step 3: Ask Jesus to take away the bad feelings related to the hurt.

Children might find it helpful to imagine Jesus standing next to them and giving these feelings to Jesus. Other kids might imagine a heavy rucksack on their backs full of all their bad and upsetting feelings. They empty it out with Jesus at the cross. When the feelings have gone, thank Jesus and pray for the other person to be blessed.

If a child has hurt others, help them think through what they can do to put things right. After praying in this way with our kids, they often made a quick phone call to a friend to apologise for their part in an argument or fight. Each time, they were visibly relieved when things were finally set in order.

Anna (8) prays the reactions prayers

Anna has had a bad day. She fought with her neighbour, Sienna, and they called each other names. Her Dad notices she is looking cross and she tells him what happened. After listening and talking at a general level about what happened, he asks Anna if she wants to talk to Jesus about it as well. She says she does and they go through the hurts prayers together. The conversation below is an example of what it might look like for Anna's dad to help her move on to deal with her reactions to the situation using the reactions prayers.

Dad: Would you like to tell Jesus how you feel about Sienna?

Anna: Yes I would. Hey Jesus, I feel bad because Sienna said I was stupid. I hate her. That's why I called her horrible names back!

Dad: What Sienna said was not nice. It hurt you! But you said some horrible things too. Why don't you say sorry to Jesus for what you said and for hating Sienna. He wants to forgive you for your part.

Anna: Ok. Please forgive me Lord Jesus for calling Sienna a fat cow. I am sorry for hating her.

Dad: The Bible says in 1 John 1:9 that God forgives us when we ask him!

Anna: I know, I remember that. You know Dad, I feel better, but I still hate Sienna a bit.

Dad: You could ask Jesus to take this hate away...

Anna: Ok. Please Lord Jesus take this hate away. I want to be friends with Sienna again.

Dad: How do you feel now?

Anna: I don't hate Sienna anymore! Thank you Jesus for taking my hate away! I think I'll call her and say sorry for what I said.

16. Jesus heals painful memories

The memories prayers

When hurts are associated with a specific incident, some kids find it helpful to invite God into the memory of what happened. God is not bound by time and space, so he is able to heal events and situations in the past.

The memories prayers are a useful tool for dealing with both simple and deeper hurts. Any pain or negative reactions which we may have felt at the time come to the surface of our lives where they can be dealt with. After a painful memory has been healed, we can still remember what happened. But it doesn't hurt anymore and we feel free to move forward.

THE MEMORIES PRAYERS

1. Ask Jesus to take you back to a painful memory.
   Wait and see what he brings to your mind.
   Let any feelings come up that you felt at the time.

2. Invite Jesus to come into the memory.
   Look to see what he does or says.
   How does that make you feel?

3. Forgive the people who hurt you.
   Ask forgiveness for your reactions to the hurt.
   Now think about what happened again. How do you feel now?

You can say ...

1. **Hey Jesus!** Please take me back to... I ask
   you to heal this memory.

2. **Please Jesus** come into this memory...

3. **I forgive**... I ask you to forgive me for...

Thank you Jesus for healing this memory!

More than imagination

When we invite Jesus to take us back to a painful moment that has already happened but which negatively affects us in the present in some way, the same emotions we felt at the time, such as fear, anger or loneliness, etc. can come up inside us. Releasing them stops them staying bottled up inside where they can act as poison to our system.

As we invite Jesus to come into a situation we try not to imagine ourselves or suggest what Jesus might do when he comes into a memory. Rather we want to take time and leave room for him to actually come in and reveal himself in the situation. Many times he enters into the memory in the form of a figure the child recognises as Jesus. He often says or does something, like asking the child if they want to play, or just taking hold of their hand. At other times, a child may not see Jesus, but they simply feel God's peace and comfort and know that he was there.

We have found that the actual revelation of God's presence and character in a memory does something to bring healing in a powerful way. You might want to practice healing of memories yourself by inviting the Holy Spirit to take you to a place he wants to heal. You might be surprised what (forgotten) situations come to mind!

Noah (7) prays the memories prayers

We return to seven-year-old Noah and his friend Joe. In a previous example, Noah used the hurts prayers to bring his pain to Jesus and forgive the other kids. In this example, we show how the memories prayers could help him deal with the same painful memory in a different way. Their prayers and conversation could go something like this:

Mum: Would you like to ask the Lord Jesus to take you back to that moment on the playground?

Noah: Yes, ok. Please Lord Jesus, take me back to this morning at school when Joe and everyone were laughing at me.

Mum:	Let's wait and see what Jesus brings to your mind. (Mum waits for a moment) Can you see yourself there? What is happening?
Noah:	I am on the playground at school. Joe says my feet and ears are so big – they're elephant's ears! Everyone starts laughing at me.
Mum:	How does that make you feel?
Noah:	Horrible! I feel ugly and like no-one likes me anymore. I feel angry that everyone is laughing at me. I want to hit them and make them stop!
Mum:	How about asking Jesus to come into that memory?
Noah:	Please Lord Jesus, come into my memory.
Mum:	What is happening?
Noah:	I can see Jesus. He asks me if I want to play with him!
Mum:	How do you feel about that?
Noah:	Good, because Jesus likes me. He is my friend.
Mum:	Can you forgive Joe and the other kids for being horrible to you?
Noah:	Yes. I forgive Joe and everyone for being horrible to me and for calling me names.
Mum:	How about asking God to forgive you for your part too?
Noah:	I am sorry Lord Jesus for hating the other kids. Please forgive me.
Mum:	Now think about what happened on the playground this morning. How do you feel about it all now?
Noah:	It doesn't really hurt anymore. I want to be friends with the others again. Do you think we can be?
Mum:	I'm sure you can! Let's thank Jesus for what he did now and ask him to help you all at school tomorrow.

D.

TEACHING CHILDREN ABOUT SIN AND FORGIVE-NESS

17. The truth sets us free

Teaching essential foundations for character and success

Many kids flounder because they have done something wrong and have no idea what to do about it. Yet learning how to put things right is an important key to character and success. So why don't parents teach it more specifically?

Part of the problem is that society as a whole has departed from God's standards of right and wrong, so we are collectively like the man who built his house on the sand. Because you want your children to succeed and be able to weather the storms of life, you will want to teach them the difference between right and wrong and what to do when they do something wrong.

The Bible calls the mistakes, shortcoming, offenses, wicked, selfish or otherwise damaging things that we do: sin. In this section, we will look at how we can explain sin to children and how to deal with it through the forgiveness prayers. They are a powerful and simple tool your child can use from an early age to put things right between them and God and them and others.

Dealing with sin using the forgiveness prayers is about taking God's way out, so that we don't get what we deserve for what we've done. And about not pushing for others to get what they deserve for what they've done to us.

The big issue

Sin is not, as the advertising would say, indulging in naughty, but nice foods. It is thinking, doing, feeling or saying anything that does not please God. Sin matters because it comes between us and God (Isaiah 59:2). If not dealt with, sin ultimately leads to death (Rom. 6:23).

A close shave

When one of our sons was seven, he raced off down the pavement taking a friend with him. The accompanying adult shouted for them to stop. But the boys just ignored her. She watched in horror as our boy dashed out onto the street. Perhaps he judged the distance to an oncoming car correctly, but the other child was watching him and not the traffic. The other boy followed, and only narrowly escaped being run over.

Disobedience can indeed be deadly. Perhaps not the first time. And it is not always the one leading the "rebellion" who pays the price. Followers can also get hurt. When we heard what had happened, we sent our son to bed without supper; one of the rare occasions we have done so. We also prayed earnestly that he would realise what he had done was very wrong and could have cost a life. After a while we heard heart-wrenching sobs from the bedroom. The experience of hunger, combined with much fervent prayer on our part, had indeed helped our son change direction (repent) and realise that he needed to obey next time.

Law and grace

Some Christians don't like talking about sin, they prefer to focus on grace. But how can we understand that we have been forgiven (let off so to speak) if we don't know what we did wrong in the first place. Forgiveness will mean nothing to us.

In the same way, a child will find it hard to appreciate God's grace (mercy, pardon, favour) unless they have at least a basic understanding of the issues of sin and guilt. The Ten Commandments (together with the rest of the Old Testament Law, with its many rules and system of sacrifices) was given for this reason: First, to show us what God expects if we want to do things our way. Second, to emphasise that we really have *zero* chance of making it on our own. When we realise the seriousness of our predicament, we are in a position to receive God's solution, his *grace,* whereby he says in effect: "It's OK. Jesus has got this. He's sorted it out for you on the cross."

Exercises to help children understand sin

Understanding God's standards

1. Go through the 10 Commandments listed in Exodus 20 together.

2. Talk about: which have we kept, which have we broken? Explain that in all honesty, none of us have kept them all; In fact, we all mess up at the first one: *"you shall have no gods before me...."* A 'god' is something, or someone, we put first in our lives, look up to and adore. All of us have put other people, things etc. in such a place in our hearts.

Showing we've all done something wrong

1. Sit with your eyes closed and fists clenched. Explain that you are going to name different sins (define 'sin' as 'anything we say, think, do or feel that God does not like'). If you have ever done it, open one finger.

2. Name sins common to children, e.g. disobeying parents, saying something untrue (lying), taking something that isn't yours (stealing), hating someone, wanting something someone else has (coveting).

3. Open your eyes. How many fingers have you both opened? If you've been honest, you'll each have at least one finger uncurled.

4. Explain: Look how many fingers we both have open! That is what the Bible means when it says that we have all sinned. It means we have all done something wrong at some time. Even just one wrong thing is like a piece of dirt in a clean glass of water – it is enough to make the whole glass of water dirty. So it is with God. He wants us to be holy and perfect, just as he is – but we can't manage this on our own. We need Jesus to help us. And God says that Jesus can be perfect for us if we want him to be.

Pause for thought

Is your understanding of sin, the law and grace in line with what the Word of God teaches?

How can you help your child understand sin, the law and grace better?

18. God's remedy for sin

Helping children receive Jesus and keep moving forward

Once a child has grasped the fact that sin is a problem, we can move swiftly on to showing them God's brilliant solution: Jesus Christ!

Jesus came to earth on a rescue mission to deal with sin once and for all. To do this, he had to become an actual human being. But the Bible says he was different from us because, unlike every person who has lived since Adam and Eve, he was not born with any sin already in his system. This was because he had no human father, rather the Holy Spirit caused Mary to become miraculously pregnant (Luke 1:34-35).

Because Jesus was fully human, he was tempted to do the same bad stuff that we are – but he didn't give in. In fact, he never did *anything* wrong at all! And, as he had no sin to start with, he remained totally clean. That is why he was able to offer his perfect life for us: He became the 'lamb of God', upon whom all the sins of the whole world were placed. In placing them on Jesus, our sins were taken away from us (John 1:29). Up until then, all sorts of animals had to be sacrificed to take away people's sins. But Jesus was the last and ultimate sacrifice!

The ultimate bath: believe and receive

Jesus died for us, but he didn't stay dead. He rose again and is alive today! And we can believe in him and receive him into our lives. In fact, this is the way that God deals with the sin in our lives (John 1:12 and John 3:16). As we do this we are actually applying the blood of Christ, which he shed all those years ago on the cross to our lives now. We are saying in effect: "I don't need to be punished for my sin or bear the consequences of it anymore. Jesus did that for me! I believe it and trust in God's forgiveness and grace to make me clean and to take away everything connected with my sin."[1] And he does! We become what the Bible calls 'born again'.

1	See 1 Peter 3:18; Hebrews 9:14; Hebrews 10:10; 1 John 1:9

Daniel recalls:

"One day, when I was eight my Dad explained to me that I could ask Jesus into my life and he would come in. Later that day, alone in my room, I decided to ask Jesus to come into my life. I was filled with tremendous joy after I did so!"

There is no need to pressurise a child into receiving Jesus in a certain way or at a certain time. But be prepared to explain who Jesus is, what he is like, what he has done for them and how they can personally receive him. Pray for a genuine work of the Holy Spirit to help them understand and receive Jesus.[2]

When our third child was four and a half, we went for a walk in the hills. He saw a crucifix next to the path and suddenly announced that he wanted to ask Jesus into his life – right there and then. So we sat down on a nearby bench and he did! In the months prior to this, we had focused on telling him Bible stories (to show him who Jesus is) and just spending time with him. We were amazed at the change in him after this day.

Even young kids can believe in and receive Jesus. As they grow older, their understanding of what Jesus has done for them grows and they may want to ask Jesus into their life again. This doesn't mean they were not born-again before, rather that they have come to a deeper understanding and simply want to express their love for Jesus and desire to follow him again.

Wash on the go: confession

Have you walked barefoot around the house after a bath? By the time you're ready to get into bed, you may need to wash your feet again. But you don't go through the whole bath routine again. Rinsing the dirt off your feet is enough. Jesus likens being born again (believing in and receiving him), with bathing our whole body. But confession (owning up to what we've done and saying sorry) to washing the parts of us that get dirty as we go along (John 13:10). This is the second aspect of God's remedy for sin.

---

2   See Helping your child receive Jesus in the Extras for more info.

Teaching kids how to confess and deal with sins, even after receiving Jesus, is a key to helping them stay close to the Lord, keep moving forward with a love for him that is alive and fresh. Far from lowering a child's self esteem, confessing our sins and asking God's forgiveness is liberating; it helps us think of ourselves in the right way (Romans 12:3). It is also a key to overcoming issues powered by sin, so that a child can get and stay free.

Remember Saul and David? David wanted to be right with God deep down inside, while Saul just wanted to look right on the outside and tried to keep up appearances. David had no problem publicly confessing his mistakes no matter how bad they were: *"Then I acknowledged my sin to you and did not cover up my iniquity. I said, 'I will confess my transgressions to the Lord' And you forgave the guilt of my sin."* (Psalm 32:4-5)

Some kids worry about whether they need to ask forgiveness for every single sin to be saved. I (Esther) was one such kid. I would worry that if I died suddenly, without having asked forgiveness for *all* my sins, I may not go to heaven. My parents explained that, just as nothing I could ever do could stop them loving me and being my parents, now that I was God's child, nothing I could ever do could change that either. My salvation does not hinge on confessing every single sin, but on the fact that I believe in Jesus and have received him into my life (John 1:12 and John 3:16).

My parents told me that sin can be like a cloud that comes between the sun and us. The sun never stops shining, giving light and warmth, but it feels cooler and darker to us. In the same way, sin can come between us and God and spoil our friendship. Once we come clean to him about what we've done (he knows anyway!) and ask him to forgive us (wash those dirty parts of our lives), it is as if a cloud is blown away and we bask in sunshine.

Pause for thought

Has your child received Jesus? If not, how could you help them take this step?

How do you deal with sin in your own life?

19. Cleaning up our mess

The forgiveness prayers

None of us enjoy running around with a stone in our shoe. No matter how small the stone may be, it presses into our foot and spoils our fun. Ignoring it won't make it go away. And leaving it in eventually breaks the skin and causes a wound. The answer, of course, is to stop the game and remove the stone. The sooner we do that, the quicker we can get on and enjoy ourselves!

Asking God to forgive us when we've messed up (confession) is like removing a pebble from our shoe. It frees us to enjoy the life he has for us and stops things from getting worse. The forgiveness prayers introduced and explained here are a simple tool children can use to deal quickly and effectively with those sins.

THE FORGIVENESS PRAYERS

1. Tell the Lord Jesus you are sorry for what you did or said or felt.
2. Ask Jesus to forgive you.
3. Put things right with others where necessary.

You can say ...

1. "**Hey Jesus!** I'm sorry for ...."
2. "**Please** forgive me"
3. "**Help me** put things right by..."

Thank you Jesus for forgiving me!

Step 1: Tell the Lord Jesus you are sorry for what you did or said or felt.

Invite your child to write or draw specific things they want to ask God to forgive them for on a piece of paper, stone or stick. When they get to step 2, help them to get rid of this object, e.g. by burning it, throwing it away or floating it down a stream.

One of our sons struggled almost every day for many weeks with vague feelings of condemnation. He was sure he had done something wrong, but he just did not know what it was!

Another time he went through a period where, almost every night God did in fact convict him of specific sins. He had done some things behind our back which needed to be brought out into the open. The Holy Spirit was showing him these things and eventually he had the courage to own up. After this season of cleansing was over, we noticed that he was growing spiritually and developing his own deep faith. This showed us that there are moments when a child needs to feel the weight of their sin to experience the sweet relief of God's forgiveness. So be patient and don't rush them through the process.

Step 2: Ask Jesus to forgive you.

Asking Jesus to forgive us means to turn away from (repent of) what we are doing, thinking or feeling that is wrong and being willing to do things God's way. Some kids will go along with asking for forgiveness, because they fear punishment or want to please you, but inside there is no real change of heart.

Don't settle for outward signs of conformity! Only genuine inner change will lead to living in a way that truly pleases God. This is the 'truth in the inner parts' (a place where no one is looking) which King David talks about in Psalm 51:6. Keep the conversation with a rebellious child going and pray for them until you sense real change.

Remind your child that we can ask God to forgive us because of what Jesus Christ did on the cross. He took our place and bore the sins and punishment of the whole world: *"the LORD has laid on him the iniquity of us all"* (Isaiah 53:6).

Having asked for forgiveness, our mind may continue to accuse us. Therefore, it is important to *receive* or accept God's forgiveness. In other words, to apply what Jesus has done on the cross to us.[3]

Note: We need to forgive others to receive God's forgiveness

Jesus taught us the following in the prayer people call 'the Lord's prayer':

"And forgive us our debts, as we also have forgiven our debtors." (Matthew 6: 12). In verse 15, Jesus adds: *"But if you do not forgive others their sins, your Father will not forgive your sins."*

You can explain this using the following illustration: Imagine you are holding a small bird in both hands. Explain that as long as you are holding the bird it can't fly away. Now offer your child a lollipop or another treat. To accept the lollipop, they will need to open their hands and let the bird go. In the same way, forgiveness means opening our hands to release the other person, so that we are free to receive God's forgiveness.

If your child finds it difficult to forgive other people or even themselves, read and talk about the parable of the unforgiving servant in Matthew 18:21-35. Show them that, no matter what others may have done to us, if God can forgive us our sins, then we can forgive others as well!

Sometimes, a child may find it difficult to forgive because of the related pain, hurt and memories. These block them and need to be dealt with. You can do this using the hurts, reactions and memories prayers.

---

3   See Isaiah 53:11 and 1 Corinthians 15:3; 1 Peter 2:24 and 3:18

Step 3: Put things right where necessary

Putting things right may simply mean saying sorry to someone for our words, attitudes or behaviour. Or it may involve an action, such as returning something you stole or paying for something you broke.

Zacchaeus, in the Bible, was someone who went to a lot of trouble to clean up his mess. He was a crooked tax man, who used to overcharge people and keep the money. Everyone hated him, but no-one could stop him. He was too rich and powerful. When he met Jesus, he realised he had done wrong. He showed he was sorry by promising to pay back four times what he had taken (Luke 19:8). This amount was even more than the Jewish law required in such cases!

Marie (11) prays the forgiveness prayers

Imagine Marie has stolen a pair of earrings. Her conscience is pricking her and she is sorry for what she has done. When her mother asks her where she got the earrings, she decides to come clean. Her mother uses the simple forgiveness prayers to show Marie how she can put things right with God. She helps her decide on practical steps to put things right with others:

Mum: Would you like to talk to Jesus about what you've done and ask him to forgive you and help you put things right?

Marie: Yes. Dear Lord Jesus, I am sorry for stealing that pair of earrings when I was in town with Ella. It was wrong. I shouldn't have done it. Please forgive me for stealing. I accept your forgiveness and thank you for forgiving me! I also forgive Ella for encouraging me to take them by saying no-one would notice and that the shop makes so much money so it wouldn't matter. Help me to put things right. You know what, Jesus, I need to take those earrings back. Please help me do the right thing even though it is embarrassing.

Mum: That's a good decision! Would you like me to go with you for a bit of moral support?

Marie: Thanks mum, I'd appreciate that!

Moving forward

After cleaning up our mess, we need strategies to avoid doing the same thing again. Explain to your child that the closer we stay to Jesus, i.e. the more we keep 'in touch' with him by talking to him in prayer, reading his Word, etc. the more effective we will be at resisting temptation (Romans 12:1-2). But if the opportunity to sin comes our way again, we must actively stand against it (resist) and trust God to make a way out for us:

- *"Submit yourselves, then, to God. Resist the devil, and he will flee from you."* (James 4:7)
- *"But when you are tempted, he* [God]*will also provide a way out so that you can endure it."* (1 Corinthians 10:13)

We see what this might look like in a conversation following on from the previous example:

Mum: Marie, is there anything you can do to avoid stealing again?

Marie: You know mum, I always seem to get into trouble when I'm with Ella. I don't think she is such a good friend after all...

Mum: Is there another girl in your class you think you could be friends with?

Marie: Um... Jane is nice. I like her. We get on OK at school.

Mum: How about inviting her over on Saturday?

Marie: Okay, I'll ask her if she wants to come.

Mum: What about if someone else tells you to do something you know is wrong? What do you think you will do next time?

Marie: I'll try not to listen to them. I'll just say I don't want to do it and send an arrow prayer to Jesus to help.

Mum: That sounds like a good plan. Let's pray about it now: Lord, we pray for a good friend for Marie. And please help her not to listen when friends try to get her do something she knows is wrong. In Jesus' Name, Amen.

E.

Tools for deliverance

TOOLS FOR FOR DELIVER- ANCE

20. The reality of demonic attack and deliverance

When protective barriers are broken

Ghosts, witchcraft and magic are popular themes in children's books and films. You may be intuitively concerned about this type of material and know that evil is a reality. You may even have experienced inexplicable spiritual phenomena. But the chances are you prefer not to think too much about these topics. As a Bible-believing Christian you don't need to be uninformed or afraid:

"Be alert and of sober mind. Your enemy the devil prowls around like a roaring lion looking for someone to devour." (1 Peter 5:8)

Demons and what they want

The reality of the demonic realm is described in the Bible. We find that we are at war with the devil – but he works through his agents or footsoldiers called demons. To win a battle, you need training (including knowledge of who the enemy is and how he operates) and weaponry (suitable to defeat a spiritual foe). God provides both.[1]

Demons are essentially fallen angels and are a part of Satan's kingdom. From conception, they look for ways to enter lives to steal, kill and destroy (John 10:10). Why? Quite simply, because we humans are made in the image of God (Genesis 1:26-27). They hate God and therefore they hate us. They are at war with God and his people. But they have been and are ultimately defeated.

We believe that our bodies and souls are the main focus of demonic at-tack.[2] Demonic spirits seek to influence our will, mind and emotions.

---

1   E.g.: *"Praise be to the Lord my Rock, who trains my hands for war, my fingers for battle."* (Ps. 144:1) and *"The weapons we fight with are not the weapons of the world. On the contrary, they have divine power to demolish strongholds."* (2 Cor. 10:4)

2   Prayer ministers differ in their views as to what extent the spirit of a Christian can be affected by the demonic.

They can be behind physical, mental and emotional pain and sickness. Just as germs and viruses make us feel unwell, so demons can make us feel like we are not quite ourselves. Demons are spiritual beings without bodies, so they are on the look out for a vehicle, preferably a human body, through which to operate (e.g. Matt. 12:44; Luke 8:26-33). For example, a demon of hatred needs someone through which they can express hatred, while a demon of fear needs someone through whom they can express fear.

The way demons get into our lives can be compared to the soldiers who hid in a wooden horse to gain access to Troy. Mistaking the horse for a trophy from the gods, the Trojans opened their gates and pulled the horse inside. In this way they let the enemy in without realising it.

We need to know, therefore, how to avoid letting demons into our lives. If demons have already gained access, then we need to know how to cast them out. The good news is that when we learn to do this in good time, it can be undramatic.

Natural protective barriers

Natural protective barriers keep out outside influences which could harm us. At a physical level, one such barrier is our skin, which keeps germs and other harmful things out. But a cut or burn breaks this barrier and makes us vulnerable to infection, if untreated.

Another natural protective barrier is a God-given ability to process emotions and experiences. We begin to learn how to do this from day one. As we mature, we become better at doing so, which is why a toddler has a lower frustration level than a mature adult!

The problem comes when situations, emotions or sins damage or break our natural protective barriers. This can happen if a situation simply surpasses our natural ability to process or deal with it. Or, if we could deal with something but fail to do so. Whatever the reason, when natural protective barriers are broken, both children and adults are left vulnerable. A demon can take advantage of the situation to move in and begin influencing our lives. Having gained entry, they do not possess us (which implies total control), rather they influence us from within. The Greek word for this is *daimonizesthai*.

Once spiritual invaders (demons) have broken through a child's natural defences, they do everything they can to try to become more and more a part of the child's thinking, feelings and actions. It is as if a demonic personality is superimposed on a child's natural personality in a given area and becomes entwined with it. That's why adults who come to us for prayer ministry often say things like, "I have always been a fearful person" or "I have had low self-esteem and felt rejected for as long as I can remember." At some point as far back as the womb or early childhood, a 'trojan horse' got through their natural defences undetected. The sooner we can get these spiritual invaders out the better. Setting a child free enables them to develop a strong, healthy personality and fulfil their God-given potential – without demonic interference.

Things that break our natural protective barriers and allow demons access to our lives, can also be thought of as 'open windows' or 'entry points' for demons. We look briefly at three of the most common ones: parental disunity, sin and hurts.

Open window of disunity

As Christians we are told to make every effort to keep the unity of the Spirit through the bond of peace (Ephesians 4:3). A basic disunity between parents and fighting in front of kids can make children vulnerable to demonic attack on various levels. We prayed for one such teenager, who had become very anxious about leaving her parents alone at home to go out with friends. The root was a deep-seated fear, which entered her as a young child. She had watched her dad being taken into police custody after a massive parental row. When she went through the freedom prayers, the spirit of fear left her. As a result she has been able to trust God to take care of her parents and go out normally with other kids her age.

Open window of sin

Demons are attracted to sin, like flies to dung heaps or rats to sewage. Anything which we know to be sinful but insist on doing, thinking or saying, can open us up to a demon that will increase the power of that sin in our life. We believe this is what happened in the example of King Saul. He persisted in an attitude of pride and rebellion towards God and hatred of David and ended up tormented by a demonic spirit (1 Samuel 16:14). Likewise, Judas Iscariot was in the habit of stealing from the disciples' money bag. This weakened his natural defences to a point where Satan was able to enter him (John 12:6; Luke 22:3).

The danger of allowing demons access to our lives through persistent, deliberate sin is, therefore, very real – another reason why it is so important to teach children to deal quickly with sin as we saw in the previous section. We have prayed for teenagers to be set free from lying spirits, which came in through choosing lies to avoid confrontation.

Open window of hurts and traumas

Anything that wounds or crushes us so deeply that it goes beyond our natural ability to process can be an entry point for a demon, which will ride in on the hurt and our reactions to the hurt.

Rejection, is a big area of hurt which can open children to demons of rejection (as early as in the womb). These will increase: feelings of rejection, self-rejecting and rejection of others. We prayed with many children in Argentina who had been rejected or abandoned by one or both parents. When they received healing and comfort for the pain of rejection, and were subsequently set free from spirits of rejection, they gained new self-confidence and were less aggressive towards others.

Neglect is a kind of collective state of hurt and trauma, which, like rejection, can open the door to demonic powers in a child's life. Neglect can mean that basic needs are not met, but can also take the form of emotional neglect, for example, where parents are constantly working or where a child is pushed towards independence without adequate emotional support or guidance.

Anita (6)

Anita had a home of sorts. But was left to fend for herself at almost every other level. She started coming to one of our satellite Sunday schools in a poor part of Salta. She was dirty, her hair a tangled mess and she was extremely restless. Anita would take off in the middle of a Bible lesson, or suddenly strike out and hit the child sitting next to her. One of our Sunday school teachers had a great love for Anita and was able to hold her for a few moments at a time on her knee before she disappeared off again. As she held her, she would pray quietly, commanding the spirits to release Anita and asking Jesus to heal her wounded heart. As the months went by, we began to see a gradual change as Anita became calmer and stayed in the meetings for longer. Eventually, she was able to attend a whole kids weekend away – without running away or hitting another child! Jesus had begun to heal the child no-one wanted and set her free through love and prayer.

Yannick (10)

Yannick was being mobbed at school. His teacher didn't take it seriously and his parents' advice didn't seem to be helping. He had become unusually aggressive at home, and had told his parents several times that he thought he would go to hell when he died. Both committed Christians, they knew that Yannick also loved and followed the Lord and was mature beyond his years in many ways. They couldn't understand where this idea and behaviour was coming from and brought him to see us.

As we talked, it became apparent that the anger and hatred he felt inside towards the other kids and teacher was so strong, that it was fuelling his aggression and making him hurt others. He felt terrible about his behaviour and concluded that it must have cost him his salvation. We reminded Yannick that nothing he could ever do could separate him from the love of God in Christ Jesus. He gave his pain to Jesus on the cross, forgave the other children and asked God to forgive him for his wrong reactions. He then told the spirit of anger which had entered him to go in the Name of Jesus. As we prayed, he felt what he described as something "hopping around in his stomach." This was the spirit showing itself. He kept praying until it left and his stomach felt normal again. Free, he went home with a smile on his face!

Note: When demons are linked to inner pain, it is often easier to set a child free if you first heal their hurt or pain using the healing, forgiveness and reactions prayers.

Other examples of natural open windows for demons include:

- Disunity between parents
- Conception and pre-birth trauma, e.g. rape, attempted abortion
- Physical, sexual, emotional and verbal abuse
- Loss of parent or loved one through death, divorce, abandonment, etc.
- Loneliness, e.g. being left alone for too long, too often
- Prolonged separation, e.g. hospitalisation, excessive day care
- Accidents involving shock or fear
- Mobbing, including cyber mobbing
- Drug and alcohol abuse
- Sexual experimentation in groups, sexting

Pause for thought

Do any of the examples of situations which break natural protective barriers reflect your child's experience?

Thank God that he has equipped and is training you to deal with and defeat demonic attack in your family.

21. Securing your house
Identifying and shutting windows

Imagine going to sleep at night and leaving the windows of your home wide open. There's a good chance you might wake up to find a burglar helping himself to the food in your fridge – with your valuables in a bag slung over his shoulder! Most people wouldn't dream of being so careless, because we all know thieves exist and look for houses that are easy to break into. So we deliberately check all windows and doors are secured at night – and gradually train our children to do the same.

In the same way, we need to be vigilant about what we allow into our homes and lives at a spiritual level. We need to learn to recognise the kinds of things that can attract demons, like rats to rubbish, and give them access to our lives. In this chapter we look at some of the most common areas we have found relevant to kids and teens and suggest steps you can take towards shutting them. These are:

- Demonically-inspired images
- Demon-driven entertainment
- Curses

Demonically-inspired images

Kids can be exposed to deeply disturbing pictures and videos, for example depicting extreme violence, perversion or demonic beings. This can happen by mistake or on purpose. As they struggle to process or blot these out, the spirits behind those images may try their best to gain a foothold in their lives through fear or an unnatural attraction towards the images.

If your child has seen something which has upset them, help them by teaching them to make Jesus Lord of their imagination and not let it run away with them. But on the other hand, be aware that they may need help to actively resist the demons trying to gain access to their lives in prayer: Ask God's forgiveness (if they looked at it willingly) and forgive anyone else involved (e.g. for showing them the images). Ask God to take away the pictures in their minds and heal any related shock or revulsion. If they are still troubled, use the freedom prayers in the next chapter to set them free from any spirit behind what they have seen (e.g. fear, violence, perversion etc.).

Demon-driven entertainment

Parents often ask whether their children can be affected by demonic spirits through certain films, types of music, video games, etc. We believe the answer to this is to learn to test and discern *the inspiration or spirit* behind any given media. It may not be immediately clear what this is. But if anything turns out to be diametrically opposed to the Spirit of Christ, avoid it (1 Thess. 5:21-22).

Kids may not initially understand why you don't want them to play that game or watch that film that "everyone has seen" or "everyone is playing." To help them understand your decision and make wise decisions themselves in future, explain to them that there are two spiritual kingdoms. God's kingdom brings abundant life to those in it. Satan's kingdom is out to hurt people. Satan wants to get us interested in him, his power and the destructive things he likes. But God wants us to love him and experience the power of his Holy Spirit. He wants us to experience joy through the things that bring him pleasure.

Beyond that, we have found that children sometimes need to be set free from specific demonic spirits they came into direct contact with through things like: playing occult video, card and fantasy role-playing games, trying out black and white magic and playing games involving asking demons questions (e.g. on-line). Hallucinogenic drugs can also expose teens directly to the demonic realm. Once they have gained entry, these spirits may work in a child to increase things like fear, aggression, addiction, attraction to evil and Satan's power. And ultimately, they will try to dampen their faith in Christ and hunger for his Word.

Perhaps your child is already a heavy gamer for example, and shows signs of aggression, depression, has started lying or become increasingly withdrawn and finds reasons to miss school. If so, he or she might need to be set free from the demonic powers directly behind a particular game, as well as freedom from a spirit of addiction. Just taking their game or computer away, without dealing with the spiritual invaders in their lives, is likely to result in huge clashes in the home and be only partially effective. After they have been set free, accompany them closely. They will need a lot of support, encouragement and opportunities to try new skills and reconnect socially.

Day-care centre kids (Argentina)

A Christian psychologist working at the day-care centre in Jujuy in the early 2000's, observed the following: the children who had begun to display unusually aggressive and anti-social behaviour at the centre, were also all reported to be addicted to a certain fantasy card game. She heard that the local catholic Bishop had issued a warning to parents to steer their children away from it, so she took a closer look at the actual content. She found the fantasy world's capital was "Satan City," and that the main character often repeated phrases like, *"I will never forgive you!"* The psychologist recognised the connection between the children's behaviour and the occult powers behind the game. It was as if something had taken a hold of these children, which they could no longer deal with on a human, psychological level. She asked us to come and pray for the children to be set free. We realised that these children had come into direct contact with the demons depicted on the cards in the game. As we prayed the freedom prayers with them, they were set free. They stopped being aggressive, settled back in their groups and their behaviour in general improved!

Curses

There are different kinds of curses which affect children. Words can release blessing or curses in a child's life because, as the Bible says, life and death are in the power of the tongue (Proverbs 18:21). Pay attention to what you say to your child and what others are saying to them. Statements like:

"You'll never do well at school!" or "no-one will ever want to marry you!" can act like a curse in a child's life which blocks them in precisely that area.

Other curses can be actively placed on a child through rituals or incantations to cause accidents, strife, premature death, sudden sickness, etc. Curses can operate through the generations as a result of windows opened by ancestors. We can be cursed by enemies or rivals known and unknown to us, or by Satanists engaged in general spiritual warfare against Christians. Families actively following Christ and those in front-line ministry are particular targets: We have had to break many curses sent against us and our kids over the years, behind things like sudden high fever and strange heaviness and depression which lifted after prayer.

Contrary to what some people believe, curses can and do affect Christians, but we don't need to fear. Remember, we are in a spiritual battle. The war is won, but the devil and his allies will keep attacking us until the end. Chinks in our armour, such as hurt, fear, sin, disunity or strife between parents make us more vulnerable to curses getting through. If this has happened in your family, simply repent and put things right. Calmly break the curse you have identified in the Name of Jesus Christ. Stand on the fact that Jesus was made a curse for us on the cross (Galatians 3:13). Determine to walk closely with Jesus again and get into the habit of pleading the protection of the blood of Christ on yourself and family daily.

Headaches improve after breaking curse

Esther suffered many headaches as a child. The doctors ran all the usual tests, but came up blank. Despite much prayer for healing, there was no real change. One day, when she was eleven, during a meeting in their home, the face of a toothless man came to her mind with a name she had never heard before. Her father remembered that someone with that name had worked with him briefly in Kenya years before. He had a bad character and soon left the mission in anger. Apparently, this man must have cursed Esther, probably, because she was the youngest and weakest member of the family. Both Esther and her parents forgave him and broke the curse in the Name of Jesus. Her headaches dramatically improved and her Sunday school teacher commented that she looked different, as well.

Teenager instantly restored

A couple brought their sixteen-year-old daughter, Olivia, to see us. She had suddenly started behaving and talking like an eight-year-old. No-one knew why. It was apparent that Olivia had been cursed. She did, in fact, remember a woman meeting her off the bus one day after school and offering her a drink. After drinking it, her personality changed. The woman turned out to be her father's ex-lover who, in an attempt to destroy his daughter and revenge herself on the father, had cursed her through the drink.

Olivia forgave her father for the affair and forgave the woman who had cursed her. She renounced the demons which had entered her through the drink. We broke the curse in the Name of Jesus Christ and commanded the related demons to go. They showed themselves and left. Immediately, Olivia was restored to her right mind and speech. Her parents wept with joy with her, when they saw that she was herself again.

Dominating/manipulative or binding relationships

God designed relationships to be enriching. Healthy relationships draw us closer to others and help us be the best we can be. However, sometimes people try to get us to do what they want (control), or use us to get what they want (manipulation). Rather than freeing us, these relationships bind us. We just don't feel completely free; it is as if we were tied to that person by invisible ropes. This can happen for example, with siblings or friends. Control and manipulation can be similar to witchcraft, which seeks to use spiritual power to influence other people and situations. Like witchcraft and the occult, these kind of relationships can open a demonic window.

A normal part of growing up is learning to give one's opinion and set healthy boundaries between ourselves and others. However, if some people have something in their lives that can exercise a controlling or dominating spiritual influence on your child, that needs to be dealt with in prayer. Ask

Jesus to cut the ropes that tie them to the other person. Imagine him doing so with giant scissors. If they still do not feel free, use the freedom prayers in the next chapter to deal with any spirits of domination, manipulation or control.

> **Pause for thought**
>
> Are there any 'open windows' in your child's life? If so, what steps could you take towards closing them?
>
> Ask God to prepare your child's heart and mind and give you an opportunity to set them free.

22. Setting children free

The freedom prayers

Jesus said that sending out demons would be one of the signs accompanying those who believe in him (Mark 16:17). So as Christian parents, we have authority to set our children free. Getting spiritual invaders or demonic spirits out of our lives is about taking away their rights to be there; and letting them know in no uncertain terms that they no longer have our permission to stay. It's about standing on the fact that Jesus Christ defeated Satan and his demons on the cross and using his authority to send them out of our lives.

As soon as a child is old enough to exercise their will, they need to believe in and receive Jesus[3] and be involved in the freedom process. You can use the steps in the freedom prayers below for this. The explanations and example in the rest of the chapter give you more background to use this powerful tool with confidence.

THE FREEDOM PRAYERS

1. Tell the Lord Jesus what you want to be set free from.

2. If it came in through what someone else did to you, forgive them.
   If it is your fault, ask Jesus to forgive you for letting it into your life.

3. Tell it to go away in the Name of the Lord Jesus.

You can say ...

1. **"Hey Jesus!** I want to be free from.... "

2. **"Please** forgive me for..."

3. **"I tell** ... to go away in the Name of Jesus Christ."

Thank you Jesus for setting me free!

---

3   See Helping your child receive Jesus in the Extras.

Step 1: Tell God what you want to be set free from.

Parents of infants and small kids have the authority in the spiritual realm to name what it is the infant needs to be free of and to command it to leave. But as soon as a child is old enough to talk and exercise a will, encourage them to say as clearly as they can what they want to be free from. If a child simply does not want to be set free, don't force them or try to break their will. Intercede at a distance for them binding the demonic spirits which are troubling them (Mark 3:27). Ask God to help your child want to be free and to give you the right moment to talk and pray with them for freedom.

Step 2: If it came in through what someone else did to you, forgive them. If it is your fault, ask Jesus to forgive you for letting it into your life.

When you ask God to forgive you for a sin that allowed a demonic spirit access to your life, you bring it into the open where God can deal with it. His forgiveness cleanses you and breaks the power of that sin in your life. This takes away the demon's right to stay.

If a demon has come in as a result of what someone else has done (e.g. abuse, abandonment, accident as a result of negligence) then the child does not need to ask for forgiveness for a sin; they have done nothing wrong. But they do need to forgive that person. Many children are astoundingly willing and able to forgive others. But if a child for some reason does not want to forgive, it is unlikely they can be set free just yet. The spirit will take their unforgiveness as permission to stay. Consider whether such a child needs more healing for related hurts, or to talk more about what it means to forgive.

Step 3: Tell it to go away in the Name of the Lord Jesus.

Imagine a teacher walking into a classroom and saying: "Would the child who threw a stone through the science lab window please step outside the classroom?" The guilty child is unlikely to show themselves and leave. They realise the teacher has no idea who broke the window. But imagine instead the teacher says: "Leon, Mr Watts saw you throw that stone through the science lab and break the window after school yesterday. He is waiting for you in his office. Off you go!" Leon knows he has been discovered. He can't hide in the crowd or pretend the teacher wasn't talking to him. He has been named and what he did exposed. He has no choice but to obey and leave the classroom.

In the same way, when we pray for freedom we need to be specific and name the spirit we are sending out. Simply call it by the same name as the problem, issue or sickness it is contributing to or causing, and state how it got in. For example, if a child battles fear after watching a scary film say: "I tell the fear, that came in through that horrible film I saw, to leave me now in the Name of Jesus Christ."

Speak directly to the problem (demon) and tell, i.e. command it to leave you in the Name of Jesus. Don't give it a choice, ask or beg it to go. Don't ask Jesus to send it out for you – that's your job. Remember, Jesus has done his part and is now seated at the right hand of the Father. The job of casting out demons in his name, i.e. on his behalf has been given to us (Mark 16:17). Speak calmly and firmly as you tell the spirit to leave. There is no need to raise your voice during freedom prayers. Shouting does not give you more power or make a demon obey you but will only frighten a child or agitate a teen.

During freedom prayers

Keep praying for freedom until the demon has gone: As you pray the child or teen may begin to feel a physical manifestation, as the spirit shows itself and prepares to leave. This could be a pressure in the stomach, the feeling that something is hopping around in your tummy, a headache, feeling of agitation, fear, nausea or physical pain. A spirit will often leave through yawning, coughing or burping, or simply as the manifestations ease off and are replaced by a feeling of lightness or peace instead. Keep telling the demon to go until these manifestations have completely stopped and the child feels better.

Thank Jesus for setting you free: Our freedom came at a high cost to our Lord – his own life sacrificed for us on the cross. He deserves our heartfelt thanks and praise! Then finish by inviting him to fill you afresh with his Holy Spirit (Ephesians 5:18).

Anna (8) prays the freedom prayers

We met Anna in a previous example. Anna has a deep-seated anger inside related to the fact that her mother abandoned them years ago. This anger drives aggressive behaviour and ends up getting her into all sorts of trouble. Let's imagine that Anna has already received some healing and comfort from Jesus from the pain of being abandoned and has forgiven her mother using the healing prayers to help her do this. She still misses having a mum, but recognises that being angry won't change anything; it just ends up hurting her more. She wants to be set free from anger.

Dad: Would you like to be free of this anger?

Anna: Yes I would.

Dad: You can tell God you want to be free of the anger you feel inside about Mum leaving?

Anna: Yes. Dear God. I feel very angry inside, because Mum left us. I can't seem to stop being angry. I don't want to be angry anymore. I want to be free!

Dad: You've already forgiven Mum, and the Lord took away your pain, remember? So you're ready to ask Jesus to forgive you for your part in keeping this anger and hurting other people when you get angry.

Anna: I am sorry for keeping this anger and for hurting other people when I get angry. Please forgive me Lord Jesus.

Dad: Tell anger to leave you in the Name of Jesus Christ.

Anna: I tell anger to go out of my life in the Name of Jesus Christ.

As they pray, Anna begins to feel a pressure in her stomach. They continue to pray until it has gone.

Dad: Let's thank Jesus for setting you free.

Anna: Thank you Lord Jesus for setting me free!

Other keys to freedom

The freedom prayers are a powerful tool you can use to set your child free. The following weapons are also at your disposal to defeat the Enemy:

- **The Word of God** (Matt. 4:4)
- **Submission to God and decision to resist** (Jam. 4:7)
- **God's commission** (Mark 16:17)
- **The shield of faith** (Eph. 6:16)
- **The Blood of Jesus and our spoken agreement with God** (Rev. 12:11)
- **The Name of Jesus** (Luke 10:17)
- **The love of God** (1 John 4:18)

23. Combining prayer tools

Why both healing and deliverance are necessary

Gardeners will tell you that to get rid of weeds, you need to deal with the whole plant. If you just remove the bits you can see, your garden may look nice and tidy very quickly. But, unless you take the time to dig out the roots, you can be sure that before long, those weeds will have grown back again. They will sprout from the part of the plant that was left in the soil.

In the same way, if we heal a child's emotional pain, without dealing with their reactions to the hurt or expelling the demons that rode in on that pain, they may feel better but not really be free. But if we combine different prayers, as you would gardening tools, we can deal with the various parts of an issue effectively at a deep level. We look at an example, in the rest of this chapter of what this approach could look like.

An example of combining prayers to overcome rejection

Remember seven year old Noah from an earlier chapter? He was hurt by his friend, Joe and other children at school when they laughed at his feet and ears. His mother picked up on this when he got home from school. In this example, we imagine that she finds out that this isn't the first time Joe and his friends have picked on Noah. In fact they have been horrible to him quite a lot recently. Noah has been nursing his hurt and fuelling it, which has made him unusually aggressive at home, something his parents had been observing and trying to get to the bottom of. When Noah finally opens up about it one night before bedtime, his parents offer to pray with him about it.

At the risk of appearing to oversimplify things, we have included an extended example of what it could look like to combine different spiritual tools. Obviously, when it comes to combining prayers with your child, you will need to respond to what your child actually says, or is or is not experiencing. This may involve talking or praying more about specific points that bother them before moving on to the next step, or giving time for emotions to come up and be released and so on. Remember, as a parent your job is not to rush a child or tell them what they should or should not be experiencing/feeling, but to be a channel of God's healing love, wisdom and grace at all times.

Sometimes incidents need to be talked and prayed about several times, particularly if the hurt runs deep and has begun to influence behaviour and thought in other ways. The prayers and examples we offer are in this sense, simply a framework you can use to help your child get healed and free.

Starting with the hurts prayers tool:

Dad: Would you like to talk to the Lord Jesus about what is hurting you inside, just like you told me?

Noah: Hey Jesus! I feel horrible inside because Joe said nasty things to me. I thought he was my friend but I don't think he even likes me anymore. He is always being horrible. I don't think anyone likes me at school. I'm such an idiot.

Dad: How about putting your hand on your heart and asking the Lord Jesus to heal your pain and make it better.

Noah: Please Lord Jesus heal my pain and make me feel better again.

Dad: How does that feel now?

Noah: Better. I don't feel so bad anymore.

Dad: Can you forgive Joe and the other kids for what they have done?

Noah: Yes, I forgive Joe for what he said to me. I forgive the other children for laughing at me.

If Noah wants to forgive but just can't, he might need to be set free from unforgiveness. His parents could suggest the freedom prayers to help him:

Mum: Tell the unforgiveness to go away in the Name of Jesus. Noah: I tell this unforgiveness to go away in the Name of Jesus. I want to forgive just as Jesus forgave me!

Noah deals with his negative reactions to the hurt using the reactions prayers:

Dad: How about telling the Lord Jesus that you are sorry that you have kept bad feelings in your heart towards those who hurt you. Ask him to take these bad feelings away.

Noah: I am sorry Lord Jesus that I have hated my friend Joe and the other kids for what they said to me. Please take this hatred away.

Dad: If the bad feelings are still there, you can tell the spirit (of anger, hatred, rejection or whatever it is you feel) to go away in the Name of Jesus.

Noah: I tell hatred to go away in the Name of Jesus.

Noah may have begun to reject himself because of the mobbing and uses the freedom prayers to set himself free from self-rejection:

Mum: Would you like to talk to the Lord Jesus about how you feel about yourself?

Noah: Hey Jesus, sometimes I don't like myself when I think about what those kids said to me. I know you love me. Please forgive me.

Mum: How do you feel now?

Noah: I know Jesus loves me but I don't like myself!

Mum: How about telling that spirit which is whispering those lies to you that you don't want to listen to it anymore and it needs to go away in the Name of Jesus?

Noah: Ok. I tell this spirit telling me bad things about myself to go away in the Name of Jesus.

Note: A child who has undergone healing and deliverance ministry, may need help in learning to walk in freedom and move forward. For example, if they were set free from self-rejection, they may be used to thinking negatively about themselves and need to learn a new way of thinking and behaving. We talk about helping children keep free and move forward in the Extras.

Possible further steps

Finally, remember that issues can be interconnected. In addition to using a combination of the five basic healing and freedom prayers as necessary your child may also need to:

- Break ungodly emotional or spiritual bonds: Tell God you don't want to be "tied" to or controlled by that other person anymore. Imagine Jesus cutting through the ropes and setting you free. Tell any spirit of control or domination from that person to leave you using the freedom prayers.

- Have physical healing: Put your hand on the part of your body that needs healing and ask Jesus to heal you (Mark 16:18).

- Learn to resist: Read God's word and learn Bible verses by heart. Try to please God with what you think about, say, watch and do. Choose your friends carefully.

Pause for thought

Review the five healing and freedom prayers (see summary on pp.142-144)

How could you adapt this example to help you pray with your child for healing and freedom?

EXTRAS

Helping your child receive Jesus

The Gospel in 5 colours

Five simple colours can help children understand who Jesus is, what he has done for them and how they can believe in and receive him into their lives. Charles Haddon Spurgeon used this approach in a message to several hundred orphans in 1866. There are many variations today. Here is ours.

Colour	Reminds us	Gospel truth	Verse
Yellow	Gold, sun, warmth, smiley faces	God loves you! His love for you never ends. He is preparing a place in heaven for you.	*Jeremiah 31:3* *John 14: 2*
Black	Darkness, marks on a page	Anything you say, think or feel that God does not like is called sin. Sin separates us from God and leads to death. Everyone has sinned, including you. You can't do anything about this problem yourself.	*Romans 3:23* *Isaiah 59:2*
Red	Jesus shed his blood when he died on the cross	Jesus is God's Son. He became a man, but never sinned. He took your sin and the punishment for your sin on himself when he died on the cross. He did this of his own free will. He rose again from the dead and is alive today!	*John 3:16* *1 Cor. 15: 3-4*
White	Clean sheet of paper	Jesus takes away your sin and gives you eternal life. You can believe and receive him in your life. God himself invites you to take this step.	*John 1:12* *Revelation 3:20*

Take a moment to respond to God's invitation in your own words or pray:

Dear Lord Jesus, Thank you that you love me. Thank you for dying on the cross for me. Thank you that you are alive today. Please come into my life and forgive all my sins. I want to be your friend forever. Amen

Colour	Reminds us	Gospel truth	Verse
Green	Grass, things that grow	Just as plants grow, so you can grow in your faith. You do this by: talking to God, reading His Word (Bible), going to church to learn more about God and be with others who love Him, and by asking his forgiveness and forgiving others whenever necessary.	*2 Peter 3:18* *1 John 1:9*

Increasing communication
10 ways to draw closer to your child

Communication is key to the healing home. Your child is more likely to open up about issues and struggles if they are used to talking to and spending time with you anyway. Make it your priority to build a heart-to-heart relationship, which communicates that they are loved, heard and protected. Here are some ideas to encourage you.

1. Start small, start today

It's never too soon to start with your child. An unborn baby can hear and be moved by your voice from as early as 16 weeks. As they grow, they can respond to your tapping your finger on the mother's tummy with a few taps of their own! It's also never too late to find ways to communicate more with an older child. If this is new for you, take small steps, like writing a note to wish them a good day or asking them about their day.

2. Be generous with hugs and cuddles

Children need physical contact, so be sure to give them plenty of hugs and cuddles from day one. While older boys may not appreciate displays of affection in public, it doesn't mean they don't appreciate hugs at home, or a back rub before they go to sleep. Teenage girls also particularly need a father's hug.

3. Read and talk about stories

Focus on the feelings and emotions the characters experience, so that it becomes natural for you to talk together about feelings. Relate the story back to your child's own experience, by asking questions like, "have you ever felt frightened like X did in our story when Y happened?" Or, "remember when you lost your teddy and you felt sad too, but then we found it and you were so happy?"

4. Eat together

If possible, eat at least one meal together each day. Sit down at the table with the TV and mobile phones, etc. switched off. Start with a prayer to thank God for the food and ask him to bless your time together. Ask your child about their day and tell them about yours. Kids like to know what the adults have been up to as well! Guide the conversation towards encouraging and faith-building topics and avoid negativity, gossip and criticism.

5. Family worship

Plan a moment each day to come before God together. We have found a good time for family worship is straight after a meal before tidying away. Keep it short, but be open to extending if discussions get interesting and children want to. Start by reading a passage or key verse from the Bible. We keep a box of thirty key verses by our table. Even after years, our boys still enjoy pulling one out and know many of them by heart. Take a brief moment to think individually about the Scripture. Then ask who wants to say something about it. It is amazing how many deep discussions we have had with our boys about faith in this relaxed setting. End by praying together, thanking God for who he is and praying for individual and collective needs.

6. Play together

Make time to do something fun as a family each week. This doesn't have to cost anything or take up the whole day. It could be something simple, like playing a game or going to the local park. But it could involve a treat or special outing. Resist the temptation to include other adults or kids in these times. This is about you and your child being together.

7. One-on-one time

If you have several children, try to do something with each child individually now and again. It is amazing how this kind of exclusive treatment can help a child open up. It was over lunch like this that our son told Daniel out of the blue that he thought he was dying. He had found a bony part on his chest he hadn't noticed before and his eight-year-old mind assumed the worst. Prior to the lunch we had no idea that our son was worried about anything at all. But having his dad to himself gave him confidence to voice his fear, and Daniel was able to reassure him that it was all perfectly normal.

8. Family holidays

Exclusive family down-times, like family holidays, offer the unique opportunity to draw closer and catch up on where your child is at. We found that these times helped prepare us, at a relational level, to survive storms around the corner and the rigours of busy schedules. You might feel like you need a holiday afterwards (things can get intense!) but relationships will be strengthened. If you like going on holiday with other families or groups, just make sure it's not every time.

9. Manage media and favour alternatives

Electronic devices and media can both hinder and aid communication at home. Managing them requires thought, discipline and regular review. Encourage creative and active hobbies, such as sport, music, reading, crafts, games and volunteering which engage your child's interest in the world around them. Get involved where appropriate, and talk about their experiences. Look for new activities and experiences you can share together.

10. Laugh together

They say "laughter is the best medicine." This is actually a biblical principle from Proverbs 17:22: *"A joyful heart is good medicine."* I (Esther) used to get uptight about being a parent and a wife. But when I realised that God is the happiest being in the universe and that he loves fun and laughter, I decided to loosen up and laugh more! I determined to laugh at myself, with others (not at them) and to find the humorous side in life. Changing my attitude diffused a lot of tension and helped make our home a happier, healthier place.

What's actually going on?

Connecting past experience and present behaviour

Reviewing your child's life – from conception to the present – can help you gain a better understanding of what past experiences, situations and events (roots) might be fueling current issues.

Making a biographical review

Think back systematically over your child's life. List any significant events, situations or experiences which were in any way hurtful, traumatic or otherwise challenging.

Start by considering the circumstances surrounding your child's conception: What was the relationship like between you and your child's biological father or mother? How did you react to the news that a baby was on the way? Did you both want a child? Did you want a child at that point in your life?

Consider the nine months in the womb. How was the pregnancy? Was there anything particularly stressful or difficult going on in your life at this time? Did you look forward with joy to their birth? How did you react to the news that they were a boy or girl (if known)?

Psalm 139 describes the unborn child as a person God knits together in the womb. They receive a spirit and soul at conception and their body is in formation. He or she can feel emotions and be affected by what is going on inside and outside the womb, like whether they are wanted or rejected. There is mounting evidence that babies in the womb experience a range of personal emotions as well as reacting to maternal feelings such as fear, pain or apprehension.

Inexplicable depression, lack of will to live, feelings of not really belonging, deep seated rejection or insecurity in children and teens is often related to circumstances surrounding their conception and time in their mother's womb. Taking an honest look at what was going on at the time might reveal the key to their healing today.

Now consider their birth. Was it natural or traumatic in any way? Were both mother and father present? What was your reaction when you first laid eyes on your son or daughter?

Continue on like this through their newborn, toddler, young child, pre-teen and teen years to the present.

At each stage prayerfully consider:

- As parents, was there anything particularly stressful or difficult going on in your lives and relationships at the time?
- What were the significant hurtful events and experiences in my child's life at that time?
- What situations, events may have broken their natural protective barriers and opened them to demonic attack?
- Were there any other open windows in their lives through which demons could have entered?

Identifying patterns and connections

Write down any issues your child struggles with today. When did these problems start? Compare your biographical review of your child's life with your notes on current issues. Are current issues chronologically related to significant events listed in your biographical review or to people/activities they were/are involved with? Was anything else going on in your child's life prior to these problems starting? Look for patterns and connections.

What now?

Now that you have a clearer idea of what is going on and possible roots of issues, begin to pray about the roots, patterns and connections you have identified. Deal with your part in any of the issues you have identified (you can also use the healing and freedom prayers to do this). As you get freer, you may notice that your child automatically receives a measure of freedom as well.

Pray for your child and ask the Lord to prepare them and give you the right moment and words to talk and pray with them for healing and freedom.

How much should you share?

As parents connect the dots between current problems and past events, they often ask, should I talk to my child about what happened? And if so, how much detail should I share with them?

If you're a single parent, the question, "why doesn't my Mummy or Daddy live with us?" might provide a natural opening. Or you might simply ask an older child or teen when they started feeling so sad. If they can't remember, offer to pray together to ask the Lord to show them when it started.

Talking with a child about painful or traumatic issues requires wisdom, sensitivity and the leading of the Holy Spirit. You know your child best, and the Holy Spirit knows them even better. Be careful not to burden them with information they don't need to know to be healed and set free. Or with anything that could put unnecessary strain on an existing relationship e.g. with another family member.

Praying during pregnancy
Your prayers make a vital difference

In Jeremiah 1:5 we see that God knows us and has a purpose for our lives even before our conception and birth:

"Before I formed you in the womb I knew you, before you were born I set you apart..." (Jeremiah 1:5).

In Psalm 139:13 and 15-16a, we find that he is there at conception, knits us together in our mother's womb and watches over the whole process. He ordains the days of our lives and gives us value, purpose and destiny. Even if circumstances surrounding the conception of your child were not ideal, God still sees your child. He has imparted his life to them and gives them purpose. He takes them seriously, as a person whose spirit, soul and body can already be touched by him and respond to him.

Healing and freedom in the womb

As early as the womb, you can begin to pray for your child as the Holy Spirit leads you. Ask the Lord to fill them with his love and presence and to help them to grow perfectly at each stage of their development. You can pray specifically for healing and freedom from issues known to you which could affect your child. Here are some examples[1]:

If you know of sicknesses or allergies running in the family, use the freedom prayers to stand against these and command them to leave your baby.

If either parent has rejected the pregnancy, ask God to forgive you for your part and forgive each other. Give him your fears and worries and receive his peace and provision. Make a decision to accept the child and thank God for their life. Pray the healing prayers, asking God to take away any hurt or pain of rejection your child may already have felt and ask God to

---

[1] For more info and guidance on praying systematically for your child throughout pregnancy, we recommend *Praying for your unborn child,* by Francis and Judith MacNutt.

fill him or her with his love. Command any spirit of rejection or trauma trying to gain a foothold to go.

If you have experienced shock or trauma, pray the healing and freedom prayers for yourself, including your unborn baby in your prayers. Ask God to fill them with peace and joy.

Dealing with demonic attack

Pray for protection daily for your unborn child. Deal decisively with any natural or demonic attack on their health or development. Here are two examples to encourage you.

Miscarriage averted

One night, when Esther was pregnant with our second son, she was on her own at home when she suddenly felt that she was about to lose the baby. She asked the Lord how to pray and realised that this was a direct demonic attack on our baby's life. She began to resist the physical symptoms and used the freedom prayers to take authority over every demonic spirit attacking our baby and trying to provoke its premature death. She continued to fight in prayer in this way for about an hour until Daniel came home and joined her in prayer. Ten minutes later, Esther felt totally normal and healthy again! As the pregnancy progressed without further incident, we thanked God regularly that he had already trained our hands for war and our fingers for battle (Psalm 144: 1). Because when the attack came, we were able to discern and defeat it.

Genetic disorder overcome

A couple received the devastating news that their unborn baby had a genetic disorder. The list of possible issues and prognosis was grim: At best, the child would have significant learning difficulties in a normal school. At worst, he would be severely handicapped and unable to walk. As we prayed together, the Lord reminded them of a neighbour's words: "Hey, you already have two healthy children, why tempt fate?!" God showed them that the fear of an abnormal child had taken root and grown through those words and opened the window to demonic attack. They repented of their fear, forgave the neighbour and commanded the spirits trying to cause the abnormalities to leave their baby. The mother felt a movement in her womb as the spirit left. Throughout the pregnancy, they continued to feed their faith on God's Word and to stand on his promises for healing – even when there was no apparent change in the diagnosis. But when their baby was born, he only had one of the long list of issues predicted, which was surgically corrected. He went on to develop normally. Several years later, the doctors announced the child was in perfect health and closed his file.

Adapting prayers for different ages
Notes to get started

The healing and freedom prayers are based on eternal truths which can apply to all ages. Simply adjust the language to fit your child's developmental level and particular situation. Here are some considerations to help you.

Small babies and toddlers

Praying for freedom for small children is usually easy. Bill Banks, an experienced deliverance minister believes this is because *"...the child's own personality, housed in the soul, has not yet come into agreement with the evil spirit. Scripture states, 'Can two walk together, except they be agreed?' (Amos 3: 3) Early deliverance, when needed, will permit a healthy development of the spirit, soul (mind, will, emotions) and body, and will prevent agreement with, or acceptance of, the intruding spirit."* [2]

We recommend praying as you hold them in your arms or over them as they lie sleeping. A child may open their eyes or wake up briefly as the spirit leaves them and then go back to sleep straight away. If the spirit has come down the family line and was not sent out in the womb, then now is the moment to pray the family issues prayers.

Young children (4- 6 years)

Pray with young children using simple language. For example, you could say to a child who is being troubled by a spirit of fear: "Let's tell *this thing* that's making you afraid to go away in the Name of Jesus." It can be helpful to hold a child on your lap as you pray, if they want to be held. This can be a way of transmitting security and love. Sometimes, however, a child might slide under the table or bed or start shouting, for example, as the demonic spirit tries to resist prayer. Quietly take authority in your spirit over the demonic power manifesting and command it to release the child.

2   *Deliverance for Children and Teens* by Bill Banks, p. 112, Impact Books, Kirkwood, 1989

Be gentle but fir m. As a demon leaves, a child may yawn, cough or just brighten up and be ready to go offandplayhappilyagain.

Prepare a young child for prayer by telling them Bible stories about Jesus, which focus on his goodness, how he loved people, helped and healed them and welcomed children to sit on his knee. Use the beauty of creation around you to show a young child how good God is and how powerful. Point out that even though he is very great, the Bible says he knows us by name and even how many hairs are on our head! He is interested in our pets and looks after the world he has made by sending rain and giving us food.

Older children (7-12 years)

A child's moral framework and fundamental understanding of truth, integrity, justice, morality, and ethics is likely to be in place by the time they reach age nine. From age ten, most people simply refi ne their views as they grow older, without really changing core beliefs.[3] Bear this in mind when ministering to an older child. Involve their mind and will and take them seriously as a thinking, refl ective individual. Help them understand the truths behind the prayers and the connections between roots and their issues.

A child who does not want to be set free should not be pressured to receive prayer ministry as this is likely to make them rebellious. If that is your child, pray and intercede for them at a distance and continue to show them unconditional love.

Teenagers

If you have laid the foundations over the years for a heart-to-heart relationship with your child, then it will be natural for you to continue to talk and pray with your child about issues even when they hit the teen years, so don't withdraw too soon! We have found it helpful to make an 'appointment' with our older teens to discuss and pray through an issue they

---

3   Based on research from the Barna Group (www.barna.org). George Barna discusses these and other surprising findings in his book, *"Transforming Your Children Into Spiritual Champions."*

struggle with. Encourage them to use the healing and freedom prayers increasingly for themselves as well.

Having said that, teenagers do benefit tremendously from additional input and prayer from people outside the healing home. Role models, such as youth leaders or godly relatives can be vital in helping teens get through these challenging years. Make attending a good church each week a priority. Chose a place where your teen likes going and can make good Christian friends. Set aside your own worship preferences if necessary; your teen's spiritual needs are more important at this point.

Consider enabling your teen to attend good Christian camps, where possible. Teens often open up to adults and each other in the special atmosphere of a camp. For example, in one camp our sons attended, the Holy Spirit fell on many teenagers, releasing pent-up pain in some, and pouring great joy into the hearts of others. Encourage teens to pray for each other as well. On the same camp, the Lord told a twelve-year-old to go and pray for a certain boy. He called our son to help and they found the fifteen-year-old boy crying alone on his bed. They asked him what was wrong and he poured his heart out. Sharing experiences from their own lives, they were able to encourage the boy and connect him with an adult team member for further help. His life was changed!

If relationships between you and your teen are strained, or even broken, it may be appropriate for a trusted prayer minister to accompany your teen on a regular basis to work through issues. Respect their privacy and don't try to pressurise either the teen or counsellor to share with you what was discussed, unless it has been agreed to do so. Your teen needs to feel that they can open up to someone without everything they say getting back to you! If this is your situation, it is likely that you will benefit from a parallel counselling process as well, to deal with any related issues in your own life. As you both come into greater freedom, your relationship with each other will improve.

Healing sexual brokenness
A framework for recovery

Most kids today are growing up in a highly sexualised world. They need help navigating the sexual minefields that have the potential to explode in their faces and leave them scarred and broken. And they need parents strong enough to stand with them if things go or have already gone wrong. Kids who are sexually broken or battling sexual sins, such as going 'too far' physically with a boy or girlfriend or consuming porn, often feel unworthy and loathe themselves.

Jake's story

Jake described how he would hang around on the fringes at church, wanting to get involved, but simply feeling too unworthy because of his addiction to pornography. We showed him how he could confess his sin and receive God's forgiveness. Then we set him free from the demons that had entered him through what he had seen. We moved on to discuss strategies to avoid temptation and encouraged him to focus on strengthening his identity as a son of God. He realised that he did not need to be perfect to be part of the community of believers and started serving God with his gifts.

Coming alongside your child

Some Christians think sexual sins are in a class of their own. The super-bad, class-of-their-own type of sin. In reality, however, it is not that sexual sins are necessarily worse than other sins. Rather, the deep connection between sexuality and identity makes sexual sin potentially more devastating, and its consequences more far-reaching than other sins, leaving aside the risk of pregnancy and sexually transmitted diseases. We have helped many young people like Jake over the years find their way back to spiritual health and wholeness, when sexual sin or brokenness has threatened to shipwreck them.

So if your child is struggling, don't back off and leave them to clean up their own mess. Don't judge them or push them away. Get alongside them in humility and love. Set boundaries and standards for behaviour in your home. Pray hard. And using your spiritual tools, pray with and help them find their way back to wholeness and freedom.

5 steps to deal with sexual sin

What can you do if you find your child is struggling with sexual sin? Perhaps they are such as caught in pornography addiction or entangled in a sexual relationship that has spiralled out of control. First and foremost, remain calm and *make sure they know you love them no matter what they have done or could ever do.* Keep the channels of communication going. Encourage them to deal with it swiftly. Use the following steps to guide them back to a place of forgiveness and restoration:

1. Confess your sin and turn away from it. Ask for and receive God's forgiveness. Forgive yourself. Put things right with others if necessary (use the forgiveness prayers).

2. Heal any hurts from related people or situations (use the hurts prayers and/or memories prayers). For abuse see "Healing sexual abuse" here in the Extras.

3. Pray for freedom from any spirits that have entered your child through the sexual sin (use the freedom prayers).

4. Cut them lose from any ties to the other person. Say: "I cut myself lose from…(name of person)." You may also need to pray for freedom from domination and control from a sexual partner (use the freedom prayers).

5. If they are struggling with sins related to sexual identity confusion, in addition to repentance and deliverance they may need emotional healing. For example if they were rejected in the womb or at birth for being the 'wrong' sex. Or if they were sexually abused by someone of the same sex or heavily dominated by a parent (use the hurts and freedom prayers).

Overcoming sexual temptation

Dealing with sexual sin in prayer is vital, but you also need to help your child avoid falling back into the same sin again. Here are some guidelines:

Analyse what happened. Help your child work out why and how they got into the situations that led to sexual sin so that they can set up *practical* strategies to avoid making the same mistake again. If you share any responsibility in what happened, say sorry and ask them for forgiveness.

Focus on identity in Christ. Build up their knowledge of who they are in Christ (identity) and encourage them to hide God's Word in their heart (Psalm 119:9-10). How does our identity affect how we treat our bodies and other people's bodies? What does it mean to be a temple of the living God? (1 Cor. 6:19) A child who knows exactly who they are in Christ is powerfully equipped and positioned to move forward in purity and resist sexual temptation.

Decide in advance. Talk to your child about how they need to decide what they want to do and be in advance; not in the heat of the moment, when their hormones are going crazy and curiosity is peaked.

Avoid temptation. Train your child to avoid tempting situations. Lay some ground rules to help them, like not hanging out alone at home with a boy or girlfriend. Teach kids to 'bounce' their eyes away from sexual temptation, i.e. look away immediately from adverts for sex toys or lingerie, or girls in hot pants walking past.

Moving forward in purity

You may wonder how realistic it is to encourage or expect kids to stay pure in today's world? After all, porn is just a click away and sleeping with your boyfriend seems the order of the day. What chance does your kid have? Isn't this a losing battle? Absolutely not! Moving forward in purity is possible, pleases God and will avoid further heartache down the line. But to be successful requires knowledge of and commitment to God's standards and the support and encouragement of parents and godly friends, where possible.

In addition to the points we looked at above, the following keys will also help you (re-) lay healthy foundations for sexual wholeness in your child's life:

Talk with your child about his or her body in a natural way. Our bodies are not dirty - they are temples of the Holy Spirit! Sex isn't dirty - it is a wonderful gift of God! We don't need to avoid the topic or talk about it in hushed tones or use strange code-names for parts of the body or the sexual act.

Affirm sexual identity as God's idea: *"He created them male and female and blessed them. And he named them "Mankind" when they were created."* (Genesis 5:2) Talk to your children about how good it is that God made them the boy or girl they are. Talk about how, as males and females, we complement each other to form a whole; even our brains are different, but complementary. This is the kind of information that some kids, pre-teen boys particularly, love - it blows their minds. And you can have a cool time researching the topic together!

Teach your child to value sex highly. God designed sex to be a powerful uniting force, a source of great pleasure and a vessel for possible new life. But he placed his gift within the covenant of marriage, to stop it exploding in our faces. Children are liberated when they hear the truth, not when they buy into what the world is saying. So don't allow sex to be degraded in your home by coarse jokes or cheap films. Be smarter and help your child see what's at stake.

Model treating members of the opposite sex with respect. Look at what love is and how Jesus expressed love by laying his life down for his bride, the church, of which we are a part. Having this knowledge in place will go a long way to helping children make informed, biblical decisions regarding their own sexuality, rather than just running (and crying) with the crowd.

Healing sexual abuse
Steps to healing and freedom

Sexual abuse leaves deep wounds in a child's soul. It affects how a child views and feels about him or herself and how they relate to others. Recovery can be a process which takes time. Sexual abuse can involve touching (e.g. inappropriate handling of adult or child's genitals or involving a child in sexual acts) and non-touching (e.g. showing a child genitals, watching them undress, showing them pornographic material).

If left to fester, the wounds of sexual abuse can have devastating effects on key areas of development, such as emotional health, sexual identity and future relationships. You can help your child overcome the trauma of sexual abuse, using the healing and freedom prayers. If you suspect abuse, but are unsure, use the following check-list to gain further clarity.

Possible signs of sexual abuse in children include:

- Unexplainable and sudden changes in personality or behaviour, e.g. aggression, withdrawal, mood swings
- Age-inappropriate sexual expression with no obvious source, e.g. in words, drawings, role-plays
- Physical signs, such as soreness, bruising around genitals, anus or mouth or discharges
- Persistent pain or difficulty related to urination and bowel movements
- Regression to younger behaviour, e.g. bed-wetting
- Identity confusion
- Excessive retreat into fantasy world
- Unaccountable fear of particular places or people
- Nightmares, sleeping problems
- Changes in appetite

If your child displays a combination of such symptoms, make sure you take a closer look. And be sure to take whatever they tell you seriously, no matter how unlikely or insignificant it may seem to you. Be prepared to take steps to protect your child from further abuse if necessary.

If you know your child has been sexually abused, use the following steps to deal with your reactions and to pray for healing and freedom with your child. Sexual abuse is a big deal and recovery is often a process. These steps are not easy to take! Give yourself time and repeat them where necessary.

Steps for parents

1.   Give your own anger and pain to Jesus on the cross.

The Bible says he carried *all* our sins and pain (Isaiah 53: 4), i.e. there is no category of suffering Jesus did not experience. He suffered so that you and your child can be free. We believe that it is probable, therefore, that Jesus was sexually abused by the Roman soldiers before his crucifixion as well.

2.   Forgive the person who abused your child.

This can be a painful process which takes time and determination, particularly if the abuser was someone you knew and trusted. Fortunately, Jesus said we can forgive "seventy times seven". This indicates that he knows forgiveness can sometimes be a struggle! It can be helpful to say "I forgive you" every time that person and what they have done comes to mind – which could be many times.

3.   Forgive yourself, if appropriate.

You may feel guilty for not stopping the abuse. But many times, there may have been nothing you or anyone else could have done to stop the abuse happening; in which case you may be experiencing false guilt. Lay this down at the cross and stop blaming yourself. If you are to blame in any way, ask God to forgive you and also forgive yourself.

4.   Ensure your child's safety.

Consider whether legal action is appropriate, and what practical steps you need to take to ensure your child's safety (and the safety of other children) in future. Your child might also need a medical appointment to test them for sexually transmitted diseases.

Steps for children (with notes for parents)

Ministering to a child who has been sexually abused requires great love, wisdom and care. You will need to use a combination of prayers, which we have simplified here in the form of nine steps. If a child struggles with a particular step refer back to the relevant individual prayer tool and go over the step in more detail until they are ready to move on.

1. Realise what happened to you is not your fault.

Victims of sexual abuse often feel guilty, e.g. "I must have done something to deserve it." Perhaps the abuser used threats or treats to get what they wanted. Clarify the guilt issues, by explaining that what that person did to them was wrong. Whether the child feels they allowed it or not, the fact is the other person overstepped a boundary they had no right to cross.

2. Give your pain to Jesus on the cross and ask him to take it away.

3. Give any other emotions that bother you related to the abuse to Jesus on the cross, e.g. fear, anger, feeling dirty.

4. Forgive the person who abused you for what they did to you.

5. Forgive parents or other adults, if appropriate, e.g. for not protecting you.

6. Say you want to be free from the person who abused you in the Name of Jesus Christ. Imagine Jesus cutting through the ropes that tie you to that person with a big pair of scissors.

7. Tell anything that has come into your life through the abuse to leave you in the Name of Jesus Christ.

Demons can take advantage of the break in a child's natural protective barrier, which a deep wound such as sexual abuse produces, to enter a child's life. Common spirits from abuse include abuse itself (which seeks to attract more abuse), rejection and self-rejection, sexual impurity and perversion, domination, cruelty, fear, panic, anger, identity confusion, depression and suicide.

8.   Deal with your reactions to the abuse.

In the case of sexual abuse, a child or teen may need to repent of keeping hatred towards the abuser. If they have engaged in their own sexual sin as a result of what came into them through the abuse, they still need to repent of these sins and turn from them. Teens may need to talk more to understand the connection between sexual abuse in the past and any demonic sexual bondage they may struggle with in their own life today.

9.   Learn about who you are in Christ.

Sexual abuse is essentially a deep rejection. Th e abuser is not really interested in the child he or she abused and what is best for them. He or she used the child to get what they wanted. As a parent, remind your child of how much they mean to you, how much you love and value them. Teach them about who they are in Christ, i.e. that they are loved, chosen and valued.

Some children ask why God didn't protect them from abuse if he loves them so much. Explain that, God has given people free will. Th is means that he can't stop them using that free will to hurt other people, otherwise it wouldn't be free will. But, when people hurt others, it hurts him too. Th at is why he made a way for us to be healed and free from the eff ects of other people's sin – by dying on the cross and taking all the sin and pain upon himself.

Issues running in the family

The family issues prayers

Sayings like, "he's a chip off the old block," or "like mother, like daughter," are used to describe a child that resembles a parent in terms of either looks, behaviour, attitudes or abilities. While we can't change certain inherited physical features like long or short legs, brown or blue eyes, we can help our children break free and turn from any negative tendencies that run in the family.

Towards the end of his life, unlike his father king David, king Solomon fell away from the Lord.[4] The kings who came after Solomon were faced with a choice: to follow the Lord or to follow in the sins of their forefathers.[5] This shows us that no matter what members of our family, living or dead may do or have done, each one of us can choose to follow and serve the Lord for ourselves. We can choose to be free from the effects of the sins of our ancestors, from the effects of sins committed against them and from any demons that have gained access to our family group as a result.

Family tendencies

We can pray for healing and freedom for issues running in the family from as early as the womb, or just as soon as we become aware of the connections. Doing so will make it easier for children to: overcome issues running in the family, resist the tendencies to sin in areas common to the family group, and receive healing from inherited sickness.

Examples of family spirits we have come across in our ministry include demons of anger, lying, depression, inferiority, pride, unforgiveness, cruelty, rebellion, alcoholism, occult powers, abuse, infidelity, bearing children as a single parent, fears and phobias and poverty. If a problem runs in your family, the chances are that demonic strongholds have been established which need freedom prayers.

4   1 Kings 11:9-10
5   E.g.: Abijah in 1 Kings 15:1-3; Abijah's son, Asa, in 1 Kings 15:9-11

We can't blame all our problems on our relatives or the sins of our forefathers. The home environment also shapes certain behaviour and mindsets; children learn to do what they see their parents doing. Having said that, *we, each of us are free to choose a different path.* So remember, we don't inherit a sin, but a family spirit can try to push us towards that sin. In other words, what gets passed on to us is the *tendency* towards a certain sin which is compounded by the example set to us by family members.

To successfully demolish demonic strongholds running in the family, take full responsibility, where necessary, for your part in continuing on in the same sins as your forefathers. And once you have been delivered from family spirits, using the family issues prayers, learn new ways of behaving and thinking in line with Scripture and teach your kids to do the same. This may mean going against what everyone else in your family group believes or continues to do. Stand firm. Freedom for yourself and your child is worth it!

Healing hereditary conditions

We have found many hereditary conditions to have a demonic component. For example, Daniel had been healed and set free from hay fever before we were married. We knew that allergies were present on both sides of our family, so we prayed over each of our children in the womb. We declared that Christ had borne all their allergies and sicknesses on the cross and that their spiritual inheritance in Christ was health according to Isaiah 53: 4-5. As we prayed in this way, Esther yawned frequently. We continued until she stopped yawning and felt peaceful and lighter in her spirit. We then prayed for physical healing of all allergies. We believed the Lord was setting our unborn children free in this way. Indeed, apart from the odd bout of hay fever in two sons, which we resisted in prayer and using a brief dose of antihistamines, they have all been allergy free to the glory of God!

The family issues prayers are simple but powerful. So, if sickness runs in your family, we suggest you use this prayer tool to set yourself free if necessary first, and then pray with or on behalf of your child.

After the spirit behind the disease or condition has left, it is important to pray for physical healing as well. As followers of Christ, we are authorised to heal sicknesses (Mark 16:18). You can pray for healing by laying your hand on your child and speaking out healing Scriptures, such as Isaiah 53: 4-5. Encourage your child to pray this prayer for themselves:

"Thank you Lord Jesus for taking my sickness on the cross. Thank you that by your wounds I am healed."

A general prayer

Knowing your family history can be helpful in determining what to pray for. However, you may not know much, if any, specifics, but you will have identified issues you or your child struggle with today. The following general prayer can help you make a start dealing with these. As more issues come up or things become clearer, use the specific family issues prayers. Just add in any information you might have where appropriate:

"Dear God, I forgive all my ancestors for any sins they committed which opened our family up to demonic strongholds, curses, sickness or any tendency to specific sins. I forgive anyone who sinned against my family and my ancestors, who cheated, abused, misused, cursed or in any way hurt them or opened them up to demonic activity in their lives. I cut myself loose from any demons behind issues running in my family. I renounce you and command you to go in the Name of Jesus. I break all curses over my life related to my ancestors. I command every demon of sickness running in my family to be gone. I ask you to heal me by the blood of Jesus Christ my Saviour, shed for me on the cross. I declare my spiritual inheritance is as a child of God in Christ Jesus. In Jesus Christ's Name. Amen."

The family issues prayers

The family issues prayers set out below can be used to help your child overcome specific issues you have identified as running in the family. Note that these prayers are similar to the freedom prayers. There is also an extra step included at the end to pray for physical healing as needed, for example, in the case of hereditary conditions. The following example gives you an idea of how to use these prayers.

Nick prays the family issues prayers

Fourteen-year-old Nick has a problem with rage. He wants to be free. His mother also had rage and identified that rage runs in the family on her father's side. She has dealt with it in her own life using forgiveness and freedom prayers. She has since been able to control her anger much better and learn new ways of reacting.

Now Nick wants to be free too. In this example, his mother guides him through the family issues prayers:

Mum: You know Granddad had terrible anger fits. Can you forgive him for opening our family to this spirit of rage?

Nick: Dear God, I want to be free of this horrible rage. Yes, I forgive my grandfather for his rage, which opened our family to a spirit of rage.

Mum: Ask Jesus to forgive you for your part in flying into a rage and for hurting other people when you get angry.

Nick: Lord Jesus, I am sorry for getting so angry and for hurting other people when I get angry. Please forgive me.

Mum: Tell this spirit of rage to leave you in the Name of Jesus Christ.

Nick: I tell this spirit of rage to go out of my life in the Name of Jesus Christ. I don't want to get so angry anymore. My inheritance in Christ is self-control and gentleness, not rage.

Nick and his mum continue to tell the spirit of rage to leave him in the Name of Jesus Christ until it has gone and he feels peace. They then take a moment to thank God together:

Mum: How about thanking Jesus for setting you free?

Nick: Thank you Lord Jesus for setting me free! Help me to control my temper in future.

THE FAMILY ISSUES PRAYERS

1. Forgive your relatives, living or dead, for passing on to you a tendency or openness to certain sins, sicknesses or other issues.

2. Ask God to forgive you where you have behaved in the same way, or for holding on to the family spirit in any other way.

3. Tell the spirit to leave you in the Name of Jesus Christ.

You can say ...

1. **"Hey Jesus!** I forgive ... for passing the tendency to ... on to me."

2. **"Please** forgive me for my part ..."

3. **"I tell** this problem/sickness (spirit) of ... from ... to leave me in the Name of Jesus Christ."

Thank you Jesus for setting me free!

For inherited sickness

Follow on by praying for physical healing.
Thank Jesus for carrying the sickness on
the cross and that by his wounds
the child is healed.

You can say ...

"Thank you Lord Jesus for carrying my sickness
on the cross. By your wounds I am healed!"

Thank you Jesus for healing me!

Helping children stay free and healed

Think like Jesus, walk with Jesus

A missionary friend worked in a part of the world where kidnappings and bombings are part of life. Our kids asked him once if he was worried about living in such a place. "I know who I am in Christ. God has given me authority to do a specific job. People are not in authority over me, neither do they control my destiny. So no, I'm not worried," he answered. This statement may sound glib or naive at first glance, but it is actually rooted in a powerful understanding of the identity and authority we have as followers of Christ.

Kids don't need to travel to remote and dangerous locations to be at risk. As we have seen throughout this book, they face enough hurt and spiritual attack at home. We have offered insights and powerful tools for dealing with issues in each of these areas in this book, but to stay free and keep moving forward with Jesus, your child also needs to know:

- Who they are in Christ (identity).
- Their authority, based on their identity in Christ.
- How to live every day in the power of the Holy Spirit.

Identity

The story is told of a rescued baby condor. He grows up scratching around in a chicken pen in an Andean village. One day, another condor glides overhead and something within the young condor stirs. He begins to spread his wings and finds himself rising off the ground, higher and higher until he is flying. Before long, he has left the miserable chicken coop, his home for so long, far behind. Suddenly everything makes sense. "No wonder I never felt like I belonged there," he says to himself. "I never was a chicken, destined for the cooking pot. I was a condor all along, made to soar!"

The Devil will do all he can to keep children from understanding who they are in Christ. He wants to keep them pecking at the ground, looking for scraps – when in reality, they are King's Kids: spiritually alive to God, in direct relationship with Him, a temple of the Holy Spirit, having the mind of Christ and all Heaven's riches available to them, destined to fly!

Your child may have begun to believe lies about themselves as a result of those same situations and experiences from which they have been healed and set free. Their mind needs to learn to think right thoughts. The Bible calls this process the renewing of our minds (Romans 12:2). As a child's mind is renewed, they get into the habit of thinking and believing what God says about them rather than the lies the devil feeds them. Select relevant key verses. Learn them by heart and practice speaking them out together.

Key verses on identity:

- God loves me (John 3:16)
- God has forgiven me / I am a child of God (1 John 1:9 / John 1:12)
- Christ Jesus lives in me (Gal. 2:20)
- Nothing can separate me from the love of God (Rom. 8:35-39)
- God protects me (Psalm 144:2)
- God takes away my fear (Psalm 22:24)
- God heals me (Psalm 103:3)
- God comforts me (Isa. 57:18)
- God receives me (Psalm 27:10)
- God is for me (Rom. 8:31)
- God never gives up on me (Deut. 4:31)
- I can do all things through Christ (Phil. 4:13)

Note: Identity is not to be confused with gifts and calling. God has given each child gifts and skills, often related to what he has prepared for them to do in life (calling). A child needs a strong spiritual identity – based on God's Word and what he says about them to fulfil their calling. But they also need to discover who they are, what they are good at and where their interests lie on a natural, human level by trying as many different activities and skills as possible.

Authority

A caretaker in charge of a big building can usually be heard a mile away by the sound of the big bunch of keys jangling from his belt! But he needs the keys to lock and unlock rooms. In the same way, Jesus gave us a job to do in his kingdom and the corresponding keys to get it done. He declared: *"what we bind on earth is bound in heaven"* (Matthew 16:19). Let this sink in for a moment: our word has so much authority and power behind it, that we can actually bind something – without physically lifting a finger or exerting any force.

As well as teaching children to use the name of Jesus, teach them the following Scriptures and encourage them to speak them out in times of trouble:

* *"No weapon that is formed against you will prevail"* (Isaiah 54:17a)
* *"...no harm will overtake you, no disaster will come near your tent."* (Psalm 91:10)

Everyday application of identity and authority

From an early age, we taught our children their authority and identity in Christ. We showed them how to exercise their authority from a place of identity in everyday situations, such as: When our boys were sick, we taught them that they had authority directly from Jesus to heal sickness in his Name. We encouraged them to pray for themselves and others for healing. If a demonic spirit had got into their life, we showed them that they had authority directly from Jesus to cast it out (Mark 16). If they came under condemnation for sins they had already confessed, we reminded them that their sin was forgiven because of God's faithfulness (1 John 1:9). This empowered them to keep free and healed.

We also trained our boys to take care in the natural, whilst relying on the Holy Spirit for protection as well. We explained to them that the Holy

Spirit will warn us of danger and we need to be listening. He can prompt us to leave a place, cross to the other side of the street or to avoid a certain situation. We shared our own experiences of practising this approach, like when Esther was a student cycling home late at night. She had a sudden urge to move into the middle of the road and did so immediately. And as she looked to her left, she saw a man at the exact place she would have passed had she kept going straight. She knew that the Holy Spirit had warned her and thanked God for his protection.

Keeping on receiving from God

When a child receives Jesus, they receive the Spirit of God into their lives and are born again. But in Ephesians 5:18, Christians are told *"be filled with the Spirit."* The Greek words used here imply an on-going process. Just as a child snuggles up regularly to a parent for love, comfort, warmth, to hear a story, to talk about something, or just because they like being with them, so we too can come to our heavenly Father and receive again and again from him. This is a key, not only to receiving deeper healing and freedom, but also to staying healed and free and moving forward with Jesus.

You can encourage your child to keep on being filled with the Holy Spirit by simply saying: *"Dear God, please fill me afresh with your Holy Spirit. Thank you for giving him to me!"*

A daily prayer to stay close to God

"Lord Jesus Christ, Thank you that you love me. I want to stay close to you today! I want you to be boss (Lord) of every part of my life – what I think and what I feel. I want to do what pleases you. I make you Lord (boss) of my things, my friendships, my school work, my future and my past. I want you to follow and obey you with everything I am. Please help me to stay close to you today. Amen."

Bibliography / recommended reading

Anderson, Neil T. and Pete and Sue Vander Hook *Spiritual Protection for Your Children: Helping Your Children and Family Find Their Identity, Freedom and Security in Christ*, Gospel Light ,1997

Banks, Bill *Deliverance for children and teens*, Impact Christian Books, Kirkwood, 1989

Gibson, Noel and Phyl *Deliver our Children from the Evil One* Sovereign World Tonbridge, 1992

Hammond, Frank and Ida Mae *A manual for children's deliverance* Impact Christian Books, Kirkwood, 1996

MacNutt, Francis and Judith *Praying for your unborn child,* Cox and Wyman, Reading UK, 1988

Neufeld, Gordon and Gabor Maté *Hold on to your kids* Ballantine Books, New York, 2006

Prince, Derek *Instruction for Deliverance for children and their parents,* Derek Prince Ministries, see derekprince.org

Taylor, Albert and Elisabeth and David M. Taylor, *Ministering Below the Surface: Step-by-Step guides to effective inner healing and deliverance ministry,* second edition, Feb. 2019. For further info and languages visit the freeandhealed.com website.

About the authors

Daniel has a masters in Theology from the Staatsunabhängige Theologische Hochschule Basel (STH). Further Postgraduate Studies at Trinity College Bristol, included marriage counselling. He was born in Zurich in 1966. When he was just 8 years old, he asked Jesus into his life and was filled with indescribable joy. He has never looked back.

Esther was born in Kenya in 1973, and moved to England when she was seven. She studied Hispanic and African studies at Birmingham University, and has a Post Graduate Certificate in Teaching from the University of Bristol. She gave her life to Christ as a young girl, but a vision of Jesus dying for her on the cross when she was 18 changed her life.

Daniel and Esther were married in 1995, having known each other most of their lives, thanks to the long-standing friendship between their mothers.

From 1998-2008, Daniel and Esther worked as mission partners in Northern Argentina. During this time they gained valuable experience and insight into how to minister healing and freedom effectively to children and teens. They initiated a series of healing encounters for kids, and saw dramatic changes in those who attended.

Their three sons were born in Salta, Argentina. In 2008, the family moved to Switzerland to give the children a chance to put down roots in their home culture and pursue their education.

Daniel and Esther founded Bethesda Heilungsdienst in 2013, to help people become emotionally, spiritually and physically whole in Christ. After more than twenty years of praying for healing and freedom in different contexts with people of all ages around the globe, they are more convinced than ever that children need healing and deliverance prayers.

Spiritual tools for kids & teens

THE HURTS PRAYERS

1. Tell Jesus what is hurting you or why you feel sad inside.

2. Ask Jesus to heal your pain and make it better.
   (Put your hand on your heart as you do this).

3. Forgive the person who has hurt you.
   (Clench your fist. Then as you open it say, "I forgive you").

You can say ...

1. "**Hey Jesus**! I feel hurt because ..."

2. "**Please** Lord Jesus heal my heart."

3. "**I forgive** ... for what they did /what they said to me."

Thank you Jesus for healing my hurt!

THE REACTIONS PRAYERS

1. Tell Jesus how you feel about what happened.
   Tell him if you said or did something wrong because you were hurt.

2. Ask Jesus to forgive you for holding on to these feelings.
   Say sorry for doing or saying wrong things.

3. Ask Jesus to take away the bad feelings related to the hurt.

You can say ...

1. "**Hey Jesus**! I feel... inside because of ... I did/I said... because I was hurt."

2. "**Please** forgive me Jesus for holding on to these feelings and for doing or saying wrong things."

3. "**I ask** you to take away this feeling of..."

Thank you Jesus for forgiving me and taking these feelings away!

THE MEMORIES PRAYERS

1. Ask Jesus to take you back to a painful memory.
    Wait and see what he brings to your mind.
    Let any feelings come up that you felt at the time.

2. Invite Jesus to come into the memory.
    Look to see what he does or says.
    How does that make you feel?

3. Forgive the people who hurt you.
    Ask forgiveness for your reactions to the hurt.
    Now think about what happened again. How do you feel now?

You can say ...

1. **Hey Jesus!** Please take me back to... I ask
    you to heal this memory.

2. **Please Jesus** come into this memory...

3. **I forgive**... I ask you to forgive me for...

Thank you Jesus for healing this memory!

THE FORGIVENESS PRAYERS

1. Tell the Lord Jesus you are sorry for what you did or said or felt.

2. Ask Jesus to forgive you.

3. Put things right with others where necessary.

You can say ...

1. "**Hey Jesus**! I'm sorry for ...."

2. "**Please** forgive me"

3. "**Help me** put things right by..."

Thank you Jesus for forgiving me!

THE FREEDOM PRAYERS

1. Tell the Lord Jesus what you want to be set free from.

2. If it came in through what someone else did to you, forgive them.
   If it is your fault, ask Jesus to forgive you for letting it into your life.

3. Tell it to go away in the Name of the Lord Jesus.

You can say ...

1. **"Hey Jesus!** I want to be free from.... "

2. **"Please** forgive me for..."

3. **"I tell** ... to go away in the Name of Jesus Christ."

Thank you Jesus for setting me free!

Online info and ministry details

- Up-to-date contact info for partners
- Order further copies of this book or find a local distributor
- Seminar and workshop info
- Supporting this ministry with donations

www.bethesda-heilungsdienst.ch

9 783952 512708